My
Pink
Champagne
Life

My
Pink
Champagne
Life

MEREDITH SHAFER

TATE PUBLISHING
AND ENTERPRISES, LLC

Published by Tate Publishing & Enterprises, LLC
127 E. Trade Center Terrace | Mustang, Oklahoma 73064 USA
1.888.361.9473 | www.tatepublishing.com

Tate Publishing is committed to excellence in the publishing industry. The company reflects the philosophy established by the founders, based on Psalm 68:11,
"The Lord gave the word and great was the company of those who published it."

Book design copyright © 2015 by Tate Publishing, LLC. All rights reserved.
Cover design by Nikolai Purpura
Interior design by Jake Muelle

Published in the United States of America
ISBN: 978-1-63449-099-3
Biography & Autobiography / Personal Memoirs
14.11.28

Shout Outs

Writing a book has been more everything—more difficult, more time-consuming, more wonderful, lonely, weird, heart wrenching, and amazing—than I could have ever predicted. I'm indebted to so many, most of whom didn't realize that they would be written about. Please take this as encouragement to be on your best behavior around me from now on as you'll probably end up in subsequent books. I'm (almost) kidding.

First and foremost, I give thanks to my Heavenly Father. My secret heart's dream since I was a child was that I would someday write a book. I truly believe this desire was planted by God, and, somehow, despite myself and all of my excuses, shortcomings, and failures, He has made this dream come true. I'm so grateful that I serve a God who never gives up on us and never fails to keep His promises!

Next, I really need to thank my whole family. To my mom and dad, there's a better thanks later in the book, but for now, thanks for always believing in me and supporting me. To my siblings, Matt and Melody, you guys are the best brother and sister a girl could have. I love you and your adorable families! To my Grandma Ginger and the late, great Grandpa Stanley, thanks for being amazing role models for every aspect of my life.

Thanks to my munchkins as well—consider this book a precursor to all of the embarrassing stories I'll probably be telling when you hit your teen years. Jack, you are the best Big Brother and my little old man. I'm so proud of you for all of your grown-upness; I'm also sorry that you're the guinea pig kid as the oldest.

Tate, you're an amazing Little Brother who is proving himself to be a great big brother as well. Now you're almost always wearing your shoes on the right feet, and you never cease to make me smile. Hold tight to your joy your whole life.

Baby Sister Lucy, you're a fiery little redheaded princess, and frankly, you don't need much advice from me on how to get things done. You're going places, sister! And finally, to my Miracle Baby, Isaiah, I'm just glad you're here for the party, my little man. You bring us all such happiness just by being here.

To my many friends, I'm sorry I can't name you all as I have a word limit. Each of you is so special and wonderful, and I can't imagine doing life without you. Many of you have caught my tears, held my hand, propped me up, mopped my brow, and kept me sane. You know who you are. Thank you for being so awesome—I'm truly blessed!

Finally, to Mr. Wonderful. Words aren't enough to say all that is in my heart. We have done more in our short time together than most do in a lifetime, and I'm proud to say that we're still standing together, hand in hand. You supported every word that I have written despite my early or late hours or sometimes leaving you with kids and almost always leaving you with a messy house. But you did the most important thing: you believed in me. You've never wavered in your encouragement of me, and I believe it's because of you that *My Pink Champagne Life* exists. You are still my rock, my love, my soulmate, my best friend, and my very own Mr. Wonderful.

Contents

Part IV: The Toast

Prologue

Bare Bones

Not too terribly long ago, I had a year of scouring, cleaning, organizing. My house, my closet, my life, my soul, my friendships. Sometimes it takes things getting really messy before I figure out I need to do something about them. For too long, every area of my life had been festering, growing grimier and germier and more disgusting with every passing day.

In the time it took for me to wake up one morning, my life crumbled and changed without warning. My then-husband decided this wasn't the life he wanted, so he went. Our house was packed to the gills with eleven years of stuff we had been unable to live without, and it was bulging at the corners and closets and foundation from the buildup of so much junk.

At the time, my soul looked similar. It was neglected and dark and frankly, only vaguely resembled a soul. I imagine it looked like a wrinkled old gnarled piece of wood that had been eaten away by fungus and left to rot. My closet was a disaster as well. As most ladies can attest to, we often hang onto clothes in four different sizes just in case we get bigger or smaller or they come back in style. Who doesn't need a pair of less-than-flattering palazzo pants? If you don't know what palazzo pants are, congratulations on not making the same fashion misstep I did.

That year of change had begun so promisingly. I had two beautiful children that we had adopted. Big Brother was four and full of pepper and shake-you-to-your-core laughter. Little Brother was just a few months old. His personality was very mellow and laid-back. He was such an easy baby and a delight in every way. I was bounding through my life enjoying my kids, my work as the director of a foundation, my marriage, my church. I was one of those women you hear about trying to have it all, and on six out of seven days of the week, I was succeeding. I could bring home the bacon, and despite being a quasi-vegetarian, fry it up in the proverbial pan as well. I had time to play with my kids because my job was flexible. Life was good at the beginning of that promising year.

Progressing through the seasons felt like, well, progress. We survived the cold and flu season of winter; spring meant Mother's Day and planting flowers in my garden and renewal of life; summer was full of firecrackers and swimming parties and aloe vera for sunburns. And then came fall—my favorite. I adore the changing of the leaves, the crisp coolness that means I get to pull out my favorite sweaters, football games and tailgates with entirely too much food, Halloween costumes, apples, and a general sense that we've moved past what people in my neck of the woods call the Dog Days of Summer.

Only that fall, it was all wrong. That fall meant leaving and yelling and shattered hearts and unexpected trauma and drama. The nighttimes, instead of being filled with the smells of fireplaces and spiced cider, were fraught with my sleeplessness. The sounds of kids playing football outside were replaced by the sounds of my own sobs muffled in a pillow to hide them from my children. The daytimes were spent wondering what went wrong, what would I do, how could this be my life? I spent much of that fall in complete disbelief that this was all actually happening. This sort of thing doesn't happen to me. I'm the superwoman that has everything together, remember? I'm the one who manages to juggle work and kids and marriage and household and friendships and make it look effortless. I'm a very efficient multi-tasker. There's been some mistake—some huge, colossal mistake. This must be someone else's life.

But it wasn't. It was mine. That fall bled into winter, and I do mean bled. My heart felt like a gaping, open wound that wouldn't heal, and the depths of winter were not helping. Why couldn't I have spring so at least I'd have flowers and sunlight and children's laughter outside to help knit me back together? Instead, all I had were short days, a shorter fuse, and a coldness that seeped into my bones and turned my soul into something unrecognizable. I had grayness and fog and my busiest time of year at my job and too many things to do and only me to do them. I had taking out smelly garbage and stinky diapers and closets overflowing with toys and clothes and crap that clogged my mind and my spirit. On the days the boys were with their dad, I had the most unsettling silence as I ricocheted through my empty house like a pinball, just trying to find somewhere to land and some way to make myself understand that this was my new reality.

In the midst of that darkest dark of winter came Lent. To me, the Über-Christian in my previous old life, Lent had been just a season to get through. It was too full of sadness and introspection for me. Forty days full of the giving up of worldly things or self or letting go to make room for the new—blah, blah, blah—it was just too much work. Those were all things I didn't need to worry my pretty little head about.

Until now. Until I was alone and broken and left. Until I was stripped down to my very core. It was just me and God, and that was it. That was how I was supposed to get through the darkest season into the Light. Honestly, at the beginning of Lent, it didn't feel like enough. I was lonely and still sad. Not the sad of the first few months where the only reason I got out of bed most days was because two little kids needed me to feed them, but I still had the sadness of realizing that my life wasn't what I thought it was.

My Lenten journey began as a quest to find a reason for why things turned out the way they did. What had I done to deserve this? At my lowest, I remember driving my car along the lake highway, yelling at God at the top of my lungs, "Where are you? Why did you leave me?" In that moment, a song came on the radio, the words of which I'd never stopped to consider before. The song was about how God works on the inside of a person, and how it can feel like complete chaos. It was all about giving yourself over to God so He could bless his way through the mess to your soul.

When I finally stopped yelling and started listening, God's warmth filled my car so full it overflowed and seeped into all the crevices of my spirit. It was like he was saying, "Hey, little girl, it's your Daddy, and I'm right here. I'll see you through every part of this, and I won't leave you no matter what." Chaos, indeed.

I didn't hear a thousand angels singing or see a burning bush by the side of the road, but the calming silence that enveloped me during that moment was life-altering. It changed my direction from asking why to pursuing the journey whole-heartedly, and sometimes, even enjoying it. Not the I-just-won-the-lottery enjoyment I still have hopes of experiencing. It was the relieved joy of one who had been so busy with her juggling act she forgot who she was and had finally let some of those balls fall to the floor.

I got to know myself because I was forced to spend time alone. I also reintroduced myself to God, putting the Über-Christian act in the garbage, along with all my other miscellaneous masks and avoidances and untruths. When I did that, I felt myself becoming real: scared, scarred, bent, and twisty inside. And guess what: God loved me anyway through my Lenten season. He reminded me that my twisty bentness was okay with Him and that He loved the real me and would be there, walking alongside me every step of the way.

After so much darkness, Easter finally arrived as the cleanest, shiniest of all the holidays. It's all white and brightness like a clean cotton baby blanket washed into softness. It's even better to me than New Year's, because as a Christian, along with the clean slate, you also get the reminder of sacrifice and forgiveness. It was then that I had myself a little Easter Epiphany. I realized that my soul had been so hell-bent on holding a grudge and wanting plague and famine and grasshoppers to rain down on my newly exed-husband that I had been holding my own self back from the new life I was supposed to be living. No one but me was keeping myself from a full, joyful, God-sized life. I had been living tiny and shriveled up because I couldn't figure out how to forgive the (pardon my French) rat bastard.

So I began the forgiveness process by not calling him a rat bastard anymore. And then I tried to be cordial when we met to pick up or drop off kids. After that, I refrained from talking bad about him to every person I ever met. Looking back, it's unfortunate that this included the mail carrier and the lady at the bank, both of whom I'm sure got tired of hearing about how he done me wrong. I went through my own twelve-step program of forgiveness, although, to be honest, it was probably more like 457 steps. Some of those were giant leaps and some were baby steps, but I was still led to a place where I could forgive. This forgiveness then led me to a place where I could let go of the hurt to make room in my heart for the goodness God had in store for me. Not to say I didn't still have hard days or bad days or days where I wanted to eat lots of chocolate and hire a hit man. I just didn't have them as often. And I didn't hire a hit man. I refuse to discuss the chocolate consumption.

Along with my Easter Epiphany, I felt something I haven't felt before or since—a desire to clean up other areas. Spring is a time of renewal, and with Easter, a time to be grateful for sacrifice and new beginnings. So I began my new beginning by cleaning up my life. My house took the brunt of it. Everything that wasn't nailed down got tossed, donated, or sold. My soul got a little refurbishing too. I started reading—devouring, really—my Bible, and anything I could get my hands on that talked about how life doesn't always go as planned or how to find blessings in the midst of trials or how bad things really do happen to good people. I spent time on me. I worked out, painted my nails siren red, played tag with my kids, watched sunsets, met friends for coffee.

I surrounded myself with the truest of true, the friends that only wanted good things for me. Those sweet people who made sure my time was occupied when my boys visited their dad. The ones whose shoulders I cried on, ears I talked off, and couches I couldn't leave until the wee hours of the morning because I just didn't want to be alone. It's amazing that when I started looking for blessings in my life, they were suddenly there in abundance. An encouraging email, a phone call, a random card in the mail, a coupon for half off at my favorite store—they just kept coming.

I'm now a few fall seasons down the line, and the blessings are still evident any time I look for them. My closets, though I'm no domestic diva, are less bulgy with extraneous coats and clothes. My soul is more cobweb free. This fall is doing its best to remind me why it's still my favorite season. I smell fireplaces burning, I hear the sounds of early morning band practice, I see the leaves on my little tree doing their best to welcome the season with brilliant reds, oranges, and golds. It's cool enough now that I've pulled out my favorite comforter and my new boots. Everywhere I look, in my new fall, in my new life, I see the blessings God has provided. There's more space in this new place in my soul because I've cleared out the clutter. I've been stripped down to the barest of bones in every way, and it's made room for all the new, wonderful, shiny-ness God had in mind just for me.

Part I

Uncorked

The Knot

My new life reads like something out of a modern day, somewhat unorthodox fairytale. Everything about the journey with my new husband, Mr. Wonderful, has been unconventional, so our decision to bind ourselves together as husband and wife mid-morning on a hot July Wednesday just seemed to fit. Most brides spend thousands on their dresses, but I wore a white sundress I had picked up at a discount store. No tuxedos were necessary since Mr. Wonderful wore khaki shorts and a nice white shirt. The two little boys who walked me down the aisle wore miniature versions of his outfit.

There were about twenty people gathered to celebrate our beginning as a married couple. The little country church where I had once been the choir director now witnessed me as a refurbished bride. Throughout the simple ceremony the little kids in attendance—mine-becoming-his included—played in the back of the church. With children's laughter as our background music, Mr. Wonderful declared his forever love for me and for the boys. My heart and eyes overflowed with joy and tears as I believed his words.

This time around, this new beginning was so *real*. I knew what I was getting into, and yet, I did it anyway. This time, I knew that marriage was hard. I knew it wouldn't be all butterflies and rainbows and unicorns when we left the church. I understood that I was putting myself out there in the scariest way possible and that Mr. Wonderful was meeting me at the scary place. This marriage thing was going to be an amazing, hard, fabulous, unimaginable ride, and Mr. Wonderful and I were on it together. This time, I knew that the pastor wasn't just saying pretty words when she said there would be richer and poorer, sickness and health, good times and bad.

This time around, it was about stepping into a marriage eyes wide open. It was about being supportive of my spouse who works hard every day for his country and about making sacrifices along with him. It was about linking myself to a man who had become my best friend and partner. It was about trusting that God brought us together specifically to create this unique family of ours.

When I was a younger bride in my previous life, I was very concerned with how everything in the wedding was going to go, from the ceremony to the elaborate reception. My first wedding was about the dress and the invitations and the pomp and circumstance. I'm embarrassed to admit that I stressed over every single detail and spent months planning everything to perfection. I had fittings and made bouquets and had a kajillion bridesmaids and showers and sent out five hundred invitations. There were bubbles and cake tastings and viewings of spaces to have the wedding. So many details to attend to that it was almost a full-time job.

This time, as a much more "mature" bride, there were no details to worry about for the wedding. Instead, we decided our time would be better spent in preparation for our marriage. We went to marriage workshops and had financial meetings so we could start our marriage on the same page. We prayed. Hard. We wanted to make sure we were following the path God had for us. We looked at our past relationships and our own contributions to their demise so we wouldn't repeat the same mistakes. We took the time and did the hard work, knowing it was just the beginning of the commitment that it would take to sustain a marriage truly until death do us part.

Instead of showers where we got everything we needed to furnish our home, we had to figure out how to merge two entire households full of stuff. Instead of a fancy wedding, we decided we would take the trip of a lifetime to Cancun, and we did. There wasn't a ritzy reception following the wedding. Instead, we all went to a *very* early lunch at the little Mexican restaurant where Mr. Wonderful and I had had one of our first dates. No flowers or bubbles or worries about returning the tuxes. Just two people very much in love, holding hands with each other and two little boys. Turns out, *this* was my dream wedding.

Marriage is a terrifying thing, I've discovered. Tying the knot is so much more than twenty gussied up minutes in our church finest followed by the party of the century with six courses and an open bar. The day-to-dayness is what those vows are really talking about. After the fabulous dress is packed away and the guests have gone home is when the promises are kept or broken. Now I know that marriage is really about accepting each other as we are *right now*, mixed with lots of grace and forgiveness.

Mr. Wonderful has been wonderful—he's been patient when all my trust issues come creeping back. Here is a man who got married and BAM! Insta-family. When he married me, he got two little boys pre-packaged along with his bride. He became a step-dad, a role he had never played before, and he's done a beautiful job from the beginning.

As if all this wasn't enough to keep us busy at the start of our marriage, we found out that our first year was also going to be filled with a whole new kind of excitement and terror. It seemed like fifteen minutes after we got married, I found out I was pregnant. So there we were with two kids already in our newly blended home and a baby on the way. A lesser man would've run for the hills upon going from zero children in his home to three in less than a year, but Mr. Wonderful didn't waver one bit. That man is built of some sturdy stuff, and it's a very good thing. Our first year together was the fastest, craziest, most wonderfully scary, hard, and incredible year I've ever had.

That first year probably set the tone for our entire marriage. It's all going to go so fast, and there's going to be a lot of bumps in the road. There will also be more incredibly beautiful moments along the way than we ever expected. I'm learning to hold onto those moments dearly. We're learning to fight better and love harder than we ever have. All of us are figuring out how to be a family, especially now that we have Baby Sister in the mix. I'm learning to roll with the chaos, and sometimes even enjoy it when I can remind myself that these babies of mine, though they'll always be my babies, will be grownups with lives of their own much too soon.

We are a total work in progress as a family. We all mess up our parts every once in awhile, but there is a lot of fun and love and forgiveness in our crazy little circus. We all contribute differently to the family. As we all grow and change and become the people that we're supposed to—

even the grownups—our contributions will change as well. This family has truly been brought together by God. We have come from all parts of heaven and earth, and we are meshing as a whole new entity. I love that my family is so unique. I love that God entrusted me and Mr. Wonderful with these kids. I love that I have been given a second chance at love.

Every day, I take in all that is my new life, and I realize, I am blessed. My vows, just like my blessings, are taken very seriously.

Life in the Hood

Colors flashing, guns blazing. Pimped out rides and rims and hand signs. Gangstas that think they're all bad, dealing drugs and being jumped in and doing time—they wouldn't make it a hot minute in my hood. No, I don't live in Compton or the Barrio or any of the places I've seen on *Law & Order*. I'm talking about the Mother Hood.

(Insert sarcastic tone here.) We have our own set of complicated hand signs and rides and color rules, like don't wear white after Labor Day. Any deviation from them can result in complete exile. Not just for you, but for your kids from the best playgroups and preschools, for your husband from the country club. Even your tiny purse-sized Schmoodle will be laughed right out of your Birkenbag. In the Mother Hood, driving a swagger wagon, aka minivan, complete with DVD players, eighteen thousand cup holders, and a sliding side door is de rigueur—take that in your bimmer, boys.

This new image of motherhood is probably stretching the truth for most of us. In reality, no matter where your Mother Hood is, it's a mine field. To make it even more dangerous, we moms don't always do a good job of sticking together. Those who work outside the home, inside the home, around the home—whatever your choice, it seems there's always someone to stand in judgment of it. Can't we all just get along?

Taking a ride through this Hood is especially dangerous when your theory of survival is the Fly-By-the-Seat-of-Your-Pants School of Thought. Don't get me wrong—you need to be able to roll with the punches as much as possible. But how much better and easier would my life be if a little planning was involved *before* I left the house with a kid in the midst of potty-training without even one extra pair of underpants? I hate getting caught with his pants down, so to speak.

Just when I think I have everything together, something happens that convinces me I don't. Maybe Big Brother's school calls and says come pick him up immediately because we don't allow projectile vomiting. Maybe it's Little Brother throwing a temper tantrum when we are already running late because he wants to wear his Spiderman costume to church. Perhaps Baby Sister has a wardrobe malfunction due to the fact that it's now leaking. From everywhere. I'll admit that sometimes it's because I've tried on three different outfits (okay, seven) but because I'm still trying to lose the baby weight, nothing fits so I throw a tantrum of my own. The Mother Hood is crazy like that.

I will say this—there's no room for sissies in this Hood. I wish someone would have warned me how gross things could be. Where was the mention of baby thermometers that go in the other end? I never saw any posted warnings that a "blowout" wasn't just for tires. Someone definitely could have saved me a trip to the car detailers just by reminding me to check for sippy cups left in a car on a hot summer day.

I could write an entire book on the things I didn't know about the Mother Hood before I moved here. I'm directionally challenged anyway, and there are days that I have felt so lost in this Hood. I had no idea how much moms judged each other. We can be downright mean! I didn't have a clue about how much my feelings could be hurt by a little kid. There was just no way to know that I would no longer have an opportunity to go to the restroom by myself for the next few years.

The fear in this Hood can be overwhelming. Am I making the right decisions? Are my kids safe when they're not with me? Should I have given Big Brother bangs? I often have the overwhelming sense that I'm stranded in a dark alley—hazards flashing, kids in the car—and AAA's phone number has been disconnected.

On the other hand, there are all kinds of amenities in the Mother Hood that no one can fully prepare you for either. This Hood comes fully stocked with all the laughter you can take. Tickling and silly games and toddlers learning to do basically *anything* can be knock-your-socks-off hilarious. There are moments of childlike wonder that are unparalleled in their ability to transport you back to your own childhood, before bills and mortgages and parking tickets and irritated bosses. You get to remember how fun simple things like bubbles or sidewalk chalk or gum or bicycles are. There's a difference in how kids view the world versus our adult view. Watching life through a child's eyes reminds us how cool bugs really are and how many things you can make with pipe cleaners. It is unadulterated joy, unfiltered, not yet tainted with the grownup-ness that we adults like to put on things that are too loud or too inconvenient or just too silly.

I'll never forget the moment I first moved into the Mother Hood. Big Brother was just a tiny baby that I was nervously waiting to meet. He was flying from halfway around the world, and my first glimpse of him was going to be in an airport. He took one look at our loud, boisterous crowd awaiting him after his twenty-one-hour flight and just started screaming his little baby head off. After the initial shock wore off both of us, I got him buckled ever so gently into his car seat. In that moment, we took one look at each other, him with his little-old-man see-everything eyes; mine full of blubbery wetness, and it was all over. He grabbed my finger, and it felt like a miniature handshake between the two of us. Sort of a "So you're my mom—I was waiting for you" deal. My arrival into my new Hood was suddenly filled with indescribable joy.

My second foray into the Mother Hood was just as memorable. I had my doubts about how this little family would go together—Big Brother was barely four and Little Brother would be a newborn. I wasn't just scared, I was terrified. Not about how people would view our very multicultural family—a blend of Caucasian, Asian, and African-American. Not even at how the boys would get along together. I was scared about whether it would be possible for me to love another little human as much as I loved Big Brother. All of those fears were forgotten though, the instant Little Brother's birth mom placed him in my arms. Without words, she and I exchanged a silent promise that this baby was in the right place and would be loved by us both forever. When Little Brother and I were alone and I was feeding him a bottle, he looked at me with his liquid chocolate eyes and little baby 'fro, and I fell in love for the second time.

All of my entrances into the Hood have been different and special. This third time around, I knew exactly what to expect once the baby got here, but it was my first pregnancy and my first time to have a girl. I also found out it was yet another way for us moms to come down on each other. Breastfeed, don't breastfeed, have a natural childbirth, have a C-section—it's all out there for discussion. But here's the thing: I'm not one hundred percent convinced we should be discussing it. I think it would be marvelous if we could all just support one another's decisions. I mean, aren't most of us trying our hardest? Don't we feel like we probably know what works best for our particular circumstances within our own families? If we truly believe this, maybe we could all just give each other a break, right?

Despite all of these landmines that can make moms feel inadequate, my birth experience was wonderful. The first time I heard that gurgly little cry as Baby Sister was being lifted out of my belly was such a glorious moment. I saw her full head of red hair and her long, skinny body and I instantly fell in love—again. I can honestly say that there is no difference in how I love all of my children, whether they're biological or adopted. That's the true miracle of the Mother Hood. A mother's heart has the capacity to stretch wide open no matter how many children she may have or how they came to be hers. God must love watching that.

Nothing prepares you for anything in the Mother Hood—the good, the bad, the boring, the long days, the short years, and all the banal in-between day-to-day things. The highs are so high and the lows will knock you off your feet. The old-timers will try to tell you. Warn you. Remind you to grab onto each moment that you can. If you do well, you'll listen. Because time in the Mother Hood is limited. You'll always live there. But it's not long before you're not as necessary. They begin to let go. And then you have to let go, too. That's so hard, and it can seem so sudden.

The Mother Hood isn't for the faint of heart. It's for the young of spirit. It's for the moms who are putting in the time, doing the hard work. It's for those who just want the best for their families. And one thing is certain: time in the Hood is time well spent.

Word from the Mama.

I Heart Cupcakes

One of my (many) weaknesses is sweets. I absolutely must spend time in the gym nearly every day to help combat this little (big) problem of mine. Besides my love of shoes, all things leopard print, baby grand pianos, actual human babies, and the color pink, I love cupcakes like boys love mud. Like the French love their toast. Like Jesus loves the little children.

It's cake's fault, really. It's probably an understatement to say I'm a fan of cake. It's my Kryptonite. A recent cupcake craze has come to town, and with all of the cool cupcake places opening, it has been almost more than I can bear. Teeny little portable cakes in sizes small enough I don't feel guilty about trying several of them? Oh. My. Goodness.

I can, and often do, indulge my sweet tooth in a cupcake fantasy. The only excuse I need is that I happen to be driving semi-close to my favorite cupcake place. What a great country we live in! There is this funky little cupcake house on 23rd Street in Oklahoma City that has the freshest, most original cupcakes I've ever had. It's an old house that has been remodeled, and all the bedroom doorways have been enlarged and opened so you can pass from one room to the next. There is old thrift store furniture and plenty of cozy chairs and places to set your feet or your coffee. It smells like I imagine heaven probably would, and it's the perfect place for some people watching.

Working there is even better than working from home. Being a social butterfly, it's sometimes hard to work with only myself and the kids for company. Especially if it's been one of those weeks where I've mostly only had conversations with small children. Sometimes I just need to hang out in the presence of other grownups and have the buzz of their conversations and laughter be my background noise. Sometimes I don't need to hear Megatron or truck crashes or that stupid toy that makes the scary clown noise. Whenever I figure out who gave it to us, I'm sending it back to their house along with all of my kids. For an entire weekend.

While at home, I have developed a very special and unique defense mechanism when it comes to the kids' constant noise: I am able to nearly tune it out. It's like white noise to me now. Mr. Wonderful is still working on this, so sometimes he will ask me in an exasperated voice, "Don't you hear that?" To which I just stare at him blankly because I was engrossed in thought or a phone conversation. Unless someone is screaming their "a-part-of-me-just-started-bleeding" scream or I hear something being flushed down the toilet that shouldn't be or there is a baby crying, it all just blends into the background. Sometimes I just need a different background.

Sometimes I need the flurry and hoopla of grownups: baristas making intensely complicated coffees, newspapers being folded, ladies' high-heeled shoes clicking across the floor, or people gossiping about work. I want to feel like I am a part of the world outside my home office and my desk. I have to connect with humans of the adult variety.

So I go to Cuppies and Joe and hang out and people watch and drink too much coffee and eat my favorite cupcake. It's a decadent concoction that combines chocolate, caramel, and—hold the phone—sea salt. Not being a cooker-type, this combination blows my ever-loving mind. You can put sea salt on top of caramel and it will be a deliciousness that the likes of man has never known? We should all take a moment of silence for the genius that is this cupcake. It makes me so happy.

I have seen professors and nurses, business people and homeless people and alternative people, students, people like myself that others probably wonder what in the world we do for a living that we can be there for hours on end during the day, and every imaginable lifestyle walk through those doors. Cuppies and Joe is like a mini-melting pot of people all brought together by the love of cupcakes. Being family-owned, you see different members of the family that had cupcake-in-the-sky dreams working every shift. It's really hard to be sad or bad or less than glad when you're there. Doesn't matter if it's raining or snowing or sweltering, it is the perfect place to spend some time to regroup. Take care of that sweet tooth. Meet friends, old or new. Relax.

Part of the draw of being in that old house is that time seems different there. The hustle and bustle of outside doesn't seem to permeate the windows or seep through the walls or come full force with the wind every time someone comes in the door. Things slow down. Worries don't seem as big and my To Do List doesn't seem as daunting. It has a completely different vibe than, say, a Starbucks. Whereas a Starbucks has its place when you just need coffee NOW! and you need to hurry up and get to work to make that important presentation, Cuppies and Joe isn't a place where you go for speed. You go when you can plan on staying awhile. It's a refuge. A place where you can actually take a deep breath.

That remodeled house has lots of character. People used to live there, and I am sure the walls could tell some stories. It's now a place of peace that refurbished old soul house. There's not a new thing in it, except for the kitchen equipment, which I'm pretty sure you have to have to stay up to code. The rest of the house is all gently used and much loved. Someone had the grand idea to make something old into something usable again. Whoever did the construction had the forethought to make a house probably formerly on someone's list to tear down into a whole new usable space. This is an act of worship if you ask me.

It's totally what God does for us, if we let him. He takes our stinky old souls that should really be condemned and turns them into something bright and shiny. He makes us usable again. He wipes away our bad stuff and scary stuff and stuff we would rather pretend doesn't exist and turns it into ways to help serve the lost or feed babies or find places for homeless to sleep. He molds us into hands and feet and thighs and backs so that we can find our place in the body of Christ.

God can take us and our brokenness and turn us into the temple he created us to be. A person that can make a difference in his or her corner of the world. I think about that sometimes when I'm working, eating, praying, watching, or just being at Cuppies and Joe. God is the master recycler, a notion that pleases me to no end.

Something old becomes new. Someplace old became the hottest little cupcake house around. Recycling at its finest.

Walk in the Light

My day job is pretty cool. Basically, I visit with people and then give their organization money. Let's just say I'm extremely popular when it's time to present the checks. It's actually more complicated than that, but the visiting and the look on people's faces when I hand them money to do their serving with is my favorite part of the job. I get to be the executive director of a local foundation. We have a grant process and non-profits apply for our funds. We give to the cream of the crop of the Oklahoma City metro area—mostly to social service organizations that are feeding people or diapering babies or helping homeless land somewhere safe.

This all means that I get to meet some of the most interesting people in my fair city. On a regular basis, I get to hold the sweet newborn of a single mom. While I breathe in the scent of that new bud of life and look in wonder at tiny fingers and toes, sometimes I hear her story while she collects much-needed diapers and formula from a crisis services center. Another day might entail meeting some formerly homeless folks who introduce me to some currently homeless people. The formers are proud to be back on their feet and now are volunteering to help others because they have walked a mile or two in their shoes. Literally. I chat with retired men and women who want to give back so they volunteer to stock groceries for food pantries or sort clothes for thrift stores or drive meals on wheels to shut-ins.

My job only serves to further convince me that there are too many hurting people out there. Even though our foundation gives grants to over sixty organizations annually, it's just not enough. Some days I feel like we're just scratching at the tip of the iceberg that gave birth to the iceberg that sank the Titanic. Times are hard right now, and the economy is a cruel mistress. There are thousands of families, just like mine, who are working to support their children and pay their mortgage and get to work on time and play hard on the weekends. And then just one thing happens.

That one thing is what turns the family living close to the edge into a family that topples down end over end into a hole filled with despair. That one thing can change a happy family into a homeless one. It's always just one thing that begins the tumble. Maybe hours were cut at the factory where they were making good money. Maybe it's an injury or an unexpected expense. Whatever it is, there are people all around us that are suddenly thrust into a life that they didn't want or expect. All because of that one thing.

True confession time: I don't do mornings well. In fact, they're probably one of the things I'm worst at. When Mama's just a little off her game in the mornings, things come unraveled quickly. I had such a morning this week, and it was the perfect demonstration of the crappola hitting the fan.

Of course it was one of the days Mr. Wonderful left early for work. Three days each week, I am in charge of all the kids' morning routines by myself. On our best days, this isn't a pretty picture, but we get the job done. On our worst days, I'm pretty sure my kids will all need therapy just to forget.

On this particular morning, it seemed everyone was moving in slow motion, myself included. We just couldn't seem to get in our groove. Baby Sister wouldn't finish her bottle at all, much less in a timely manner. Big Brother took a day-and-a-half just to eat breakfast. And Little Brother—well, let's just say Little Brother was having troubles. With *everything*. He couldn't find his pants that his Big Brother had just handed him. He dropped his toothbrush in the potty. He got in trouble for playing with his superheroes instead of putting on his shoes and socks. The list goes on.

It was a rough day for everyone. I hate these kinds of mornings because it's just the wrongest way possible to start your day. I say wrongest because that is exactly how wrong it was. Frankly, there's no word in the English language that does it justice. It makes me feel like a cranky old woman when I send my kids off to school after a morning like that.

I also have no inclination to go and talk nice with people when we get our morning started poorly. After a workout and dropping the kids off at school, things still felt crazed and disjointed. It was one of those days that I really wanted to call in sick.

But instead, I headed to a site visit at a place called OKC Compassion. I should have known God was going to teach me something that day since I was so out of sorts. This particular ministry feeds people six days a week. They offer a place to get out of the elements. Their doors open at 7:00 a.m. and close around 6:00 p.m. when other shelters open up for the night.

OKC Compassion doesn't just give away food. They have clothes and Thanksgiving turkeys and Christmas baskets and prayer. They can help with alcohol or drug addiction. They can even help navigate bureaucratic agencies that won't help you unless you have a home address and contact information to give them. This is very difficult when you don't have a home. Or when English isn't your first language.

Every time I visit OKC Compassion, I am impressed with the amount of help this little organization is trying to give. They have a teeny tiny budget but that doesn't make them turn people away. They want to help those who are hurting the most. There is always someone working in the office who was helped by OKC Compassion. Sometimes it's a single mom who was fed, along with her several children, by the lunch program until she got herself together. Other times it's a man who lived in one of the recovery houses and has been clean and sober for nine months now and is just trying to stay on the path and give a little back at the same time.

This particular time, I met a man I'll call Bob. He was preaching up a storm when I got there. Lots of people were ready to eat, but they wouldn't be getting to the food until Bob was finished telling them about God's love. And he had plenty to say about it.

When he finally wrapped up his sermon, people shuffled through the line to get a plate piled high with delicious smelling food. All kinds of people were there. Some were long-time homeless, people for whom having a consistent roof was a faint memory. You could tell who the newly needy were. They still had that scared, jumpy look, like they weren't used to wearing this new reality yet. Or were still hoping to wake up from it.

There were old people, and young people old before their time. A lot of those in line were in need of dental work or medication or showers or a hug or food. Every single one of them had their own story of how they came to be there. How they had gotten to this place of need.

As the line shortened and people were settling in for their hot meal on this blustery cold day, I was introduced to Bob. He walked with a cane and a severe limp. I could peg his age as anywhere between thirty-five and sixty. His smile revealed several gold teeth, and he began by telling me how happy he was.

In my mind, I questioned his sincerity at first. Happy? How are you happy *here*? You're getting free lunch from a shelter and you are happy? This was not computing with me. He then proceeded to tell me just a sliver of what he had been through in his life. He had been beaten, homeless, addicted. He had been shot, which paralyzed him. After several years in a wheelchair, he finally learned to hobble about with his cane.

Bob was the kind of man who sprinkled his sentences with words like dope house and cocaine as casually as I might say spaghetti or Wal-Mart. His life experience consisted of actual trials and tribulations, but that wasn't what he wanted you to hear. He had to tell you about all of his darkness so you could understand why he was so happy. He was finally walking in the Light.

As I sat in my car after my brief encounter with Bob, who I think must be one of God's angels for sure, I felt ashamed. Earlier that morning, between my exasperation with the baby for not drinking her bottle and my near-apoplectic fit when Little Brother had his shoes on the wrong feet, I was thinking the most ungrateful thoughts. I was facing minor irritations at best, and I was crumpling under their weight. My children were experiencing a Mama-meltdown.

Real problems deserve a certain level of emotion. I had three beautiful, active children, and I was missing an opportunity every morning to give them the best possible start to their day. They weren't seeing how great it was to have another chance every time they woke up. They weren't grasping the potential that each moment contains because I wasn't showing them. With all these blessings surrounding me and daily being poured over me, why wasn't I walking in the Light as well?

I vowed right then and there that I would do better. Because I can do better. I know I'll still mess up occasionally, but from now on, I'm going to attack the mornings with gusto and gratitude instead of grump my way down my To Do List. It's more important for my kids to see Mama just hanging loose, rolling with it all—good and bad—with a smile on her face than for shoes to be on the right feet or clothes to match. One of the best things I can teach my children is how to start the day thanking God for all the blessings he's given our family.

Walking in the Light is about walking with God. Through the big or small or ridiculous or three hundredth time you've said don't put toys in the potty. It doesn't matter. What matters is how I am teaching my kids with everything I do and everything I am—even in the morning—how to be a child of the Sonlight.

Domestic Goddess

Hi, my name is Meredith. And I am NOT a Domestic Goddess.

Y'all just come by anytime—I *love* company. But prepare yourself. My house usually falls into the Mildly Presentable category at any given time, but sometimes it even slips down into the I'm-Sorry-You-Had-To-See-This division. Upon walking in my front door, you will notice dust bunnies scurrying under chairs and toys upon toys upon toys overflowing their too-small containers. Disclaimer #1: if you choose to sit down at my house, you will experience dog hair butt. I'm just saying.

Please do not open my closets. Or drawers. Or anyplace that could house a large amount of stuff that could be a potential weapon if you were to remove the barrier holding it back. The last person who attempted to look in my coat closet has not been seen since 2001. I don't cook. I don't even really clean. I am pretty good at scootching things under other things, but that is really the extent of my Goddessness.

Sadly, I didn't know where the bleach went in our washer until I asked Mr. Wonderful. Hiding his grin, he showed me what to do. Not that it's a good excuse, but I never used bleach until Mr. Wonderful came onto the scene with all his whites. To further demonstrate the extent of my lack of domestic fortitude, let me tell you about when my friend Sheryl called and invited us over for dinner. Never wanting to show up empty-handed, I asked her what I could bring. "Why don't you make a pan of brownies?" she asked. To which I replied, "Have you even met me?" She knows darn good and well that this mama don't cook.

The worst part of this story—the part that will make you shake your head in wonder—is the fact that I am a direct descendant of the Ultimate Goddess in Domesticity: my mom. Think Betty Crocker mixed with pre-jail stint Martha Stewart and you get Mom Beth. Somehow she managed to keep a perfect house, raise three kids, teach French *and* math at the high school level full-time—all while going to school to get her master's degree. This meant driving ninety miles to the university. One way.

I cannot live up to that! I would have to be an actual superhero to accomplish leaping over the tall piles of toys scattered about my house. Or be faster than a speeding toddler to keep food stains off my carpet. If we are talking female superheroes, can I at least be Wonder Woman? I love her bustier with boots look, and I am sure I wouldn't get any complaints from Mr. Wonderful. That truly was a bold fashion statement, wasn't it?

With those kinds of impossible standards out there, it's no wonder I feel like I am not doing enough. In today's world, a woman's success is measured by how full her calendar is, how many technological gadgets her kids have, and how nice her house looks. Pretty sure I am failing at all of those. Is it wrong that sometimes I just want something to be easy?

That's just the beginning of my domestic challenges. So what if I only shave my legs up to my knee—have you seen how much territory we women are supposed to cover? I really only like clicky pens. No lids my kids could use as some sort of jailhouse shank. I'm sure many of you reading this will be appalled at the fact that I do not bathe my kids every day. There, I said it. That's right, I don't. I know kids get stinky, but in defense of this philosophy, their skin is very dry and they are just going to get dirty again.

I get that I am not built for the Domestic Goddess lifestyle. Apparently that gene skipped a generation. There may be a layer of dust covering most everything in my house. My bathroom sinks probably have toothpaste remnants as decoration, my dining room table is covered with stacks of magazines and bills, and if you were to sweep my tile, you could probably make a wig from all the dog hair. Leaving things be just gives me more time to play outside with my kids or take a minute for myself or read or book or have a grownup conversation with Mr. Wonderful.

I'll admit, it's possible that I know too many show tunes and not enough ways to get stains out of clothing. That is so okay with me. I know how to make treasure maps for my kids and play The Princess and Her Pirate Boys, but I haven't the slightest clue as to how to get my bathroom shower clean. I work from home, so there *is* a need in my soul for some order. If I can clear the clutter, it seems to help clear my mind. But that just means I have a don't ask, don't tell policy with my house. I do not want to know where the boys put all those toys that were littering the living room floor a minute ago. I'm just happy that they are out of my sight.

When my mom, the afore-mentioned Ultimate Goddess in Domesticity, is at my house, my worry is that she might discover how far gone I am. Mom is the type of woman who will rearrange my dishwasher for maximum capacity. She is the one to call in a stain emergency. At every house or apartment I have ever moved into, she has helped clean it before I moved in. Judging by the results at her own house, she truly knows the best way to do nearly everything domestic.

Several of my best friends are also neat-freaks. It seems I surround myself with people like this. In my professional opinion, it is probably because I am *not* a neat-freak. (Disclaimer #2: I am not able to accurately diagnose any issues as I went to law school, not medical school. Thus the disclaimer.) I am so impressed when I go to my friend's house. She has a chore chart on her refrigerator. It is color-coded and filled out, like everything has actually been completed. I could look at that chart for hours and still not have a solid grasp of what a lint trap is or how to replace the fridge filter or why you should dust your baseboards. How do people know to do all of this stuff? Did I skip that class in college? Does any of this make a difference to me or my family? Will my life be improved in some tangible way?

I think for some, like my mom and my friend, it probably does matter and their lives are improved. I guarantee no one ever took anything out of their refrigerator and asked what it used to be or found a sippy cup at their house that had been lost under the couch for eight days so the milk was now cottage cheese. I totally applaud that. It is just not healthy to have things growing in your food and drink.

But in my world, the type of cleanliness that requires a chore chart and actual cleaning is not only unattainable; it is a waste of my time. I could be sleeping. Or playing hide-and-seek with the boys for the hundredth time. Or working out. If I were to make a chore chart for my house that was fairly realistic, it would include smooching time and creative time and be-silly-with-my-kids time and sushi and cocktails time.

My theory is that in the world of the Domestic Goddess, her soul *is* fed by caring for her home—it is how she shows love to others and how she finds some of her own personal fulfillment. I think that is awesome. For her. For me, my soul is fed when I make a collage with my boys, glue and magazine clippings strewn about. It may have our dreams on it, or the places we want to visit or the things we would like to do. Or when, after Mr. Wonderful and I put all our little yahoos to bed at a ridiculously early hour, we retire to our bedroom, the Oasis. The ceiling fan blades have rarely been dusted and there are probably some clean clothes piled on my leopard print chair. We don't mind. We can reconnect, catch up on our day, read, watch television, hang out, or make out—the possibilities are endless.

There are a lot of things in this world that I just don't have time for: math word problems, listening to CNN, learning how a combustible engine works, and cleaning. To those with antibacterial sensibilities, I heartily apologize. In fact, if it makes you feel better, I would be happy to meet you at your house where I have no doubt it is cleaner. I don't have time for folding laundry as soon as it comes out of the dryer or running the vacuum every day (heck, let's be real—every week) or cooking gourmet meals. But to those of you who do, you rock!

What I do have time for is cutting out of work early to take my kids to the pool. Or dancing in the kitchen with Mr. Wonderful while he is cooking and I am sous chef-ing. Finding time to spend twenty minutes doing something good for my body or buying yet another shade of lip gloss or sipping a margarita on the back patio or sending a card to a friend—these are all things I can work into my schedule.

I guess what I am saying is that though I wholly appreciate the Domestic Goddess lifestyle, I don't aspire to it. I really just want to do the best I can to love my kids in my own special way, shoving as many memories into their tiny bodies as I can before they pull away to make their own lives. So maybe when you come over, we will sit on the back patio with a cool drink and you can just overlook my dirty house.

Who knows—if you happen to visit at just the right time, you might even catch me in my Wonder Woman outfit.

Grace Is the New Black

Grace is a tricky concept for me, kind of like gravity or trigonometry or finance charges. I love what God does with it, but when it comes to applying it to my own circumstances, I don't always do a great job of displaying grace. It's hard. It takes time or effort or putting others first. Frankly, as humans, unless you are Mother Teresa or Ghandi or Oprah, it seems that we don't have the capacity for giving away like we should.

I get lazy when it comes to grace. Even though it has been extended to me over and over, when it's my turn, I forget how to give grace to others. In the Bible, there are tons of examples of grace. That parable where the dad kills a fatted calf upon the return of his Loser Son is a good one. That son broke his dad's heart, ran away, did a bunch of bad and stupid things, then came back begging to be a servant. Practically before the son could get the words out, his dad was shouting at everyone, "Look, guys—my kid came home! I thought I'd never see him again but praise God, here he is!"

I love the dad's celebration. I also identify with the other son's reaction. Here was Dutiful Son, the one who had stayed at home with dad, doing hard labor instead of sowing his wild oats. Who knows how long he'd been trudging and drudging through that life. Was there a celebration for all his time and hard work? Nope. But when Loser Son comes home after messing up everything in his life, the dad wanted Dutiful Son to celebrate too. Does that remind you of anyone? It does me.

It makes me recall all the times when I have watched people who have done me wrong in some way, big or small, get things I thought they didn't deserve. Whereas I would have had them catching some sort of pox (small or chicken, I don't care) or going bankrupt or losing all their friends and their fashion sense to boot, God's grace is still there for them. Didn't they hurt you too, Lord? I just want to ask how in the universe He can let good things happen to bad people. In my opinion, they should have at least been required to have some sort of Cosmic Timeout.

But that is why God is the Creator of the Universe and not me. If we did things my way, the human way, there would not be an ultimate sacrifice of God's son for any of us until we deserved it—which, let's face it—would be never. No matter how hard we work at being the perfect Christian or human or friend or mom or daughter, every time we will fail to deserve a gift that huge. So it is hard to wrap our minds around God's concept of grace that is given long before we deserve it. If we ever do.

That is fantastic news, though. It means that every time we screw up, even if it is the thousandth time, God still extends his grace to us. Every time. It doesn't matter how bad we destroy ourselves or our bodies or our credit or someone else's car or heart or life. God is still going to love us like we are the Loser Son, throwing us a party when we return. He is going to bust out the grill, throw on some tunes, invite all his friends, and bake us a cake upon coming back to Him. That is all we have to do—come back. We don't even have to come back very far; it is just one step.

Grace is beyond hard. It is all about giving: your time, your effort, your money, your ear, your shoulder, your aid. I think we are probably presented with hundreds of opportunities to extend grace every day, but we just overlook most of them or ignore them or pray for God to send someone else to help that person. Usually it's not at the most convenient time. We might have other plans. We may not feel like we have enough time or money or the skills to help.

I kind of think that God puts us—little ol' us—in places to help people all the time. We're just really good at excusing ourselves from responsibility or talking ourselves out of it. I am usually fairly creative here. But God, I don't have any money this pay period and *my* kid needs shoes. Or I don't have enough know-how or time or I have three kids with me so it is just too much trouble. I have so many excuses.

Sometimes I have a moment of insight and stop myself. I think about the debt of gratitude that I owe so many people. During hard times in my life, I have always had the luxury of friends and family surrounding me. They love me through the ordeal, offering help in whatever way I seem to need it at exactly the right time. I've had so many blessings on the help-front that I will never be able to repay all of the people responsible for taking such good care of me. I certainly didn't do anything to deserve all of that grace that just fell in my lap.

I think the only thing I can do is to pass it on. Pay it forward. Let it come full circle. It is high time I become a blessing to someone else every chance I get, every day. This is just a small way to say thanks for all of the times God has put just the right person with exactly the right skill set or circumstance or knowledge or heart I needed in my path. Coincidence? No way. I cannot believe that a God who cares so much about the lilies of the field and the birds of the air wouldn't do so much more for me, including extending grace to me through others. I'm not even one hundred percent certain you can call yourself a Christian and believe in coincidence.

The people that I am indebted to are people for whom it took effort on their part. They watched my children—no easy task. They met me for coffee despite being swamped in their own lives with kids and work and so many other responsibilities it would make your head swim. They listened, even though they were facing medical procedures or had a loved one pass away or were going through junk of their own. These kind, loving people that God sent to me knew or said or did exactly the right thing. They gave up something to help me.

So now I am trying to be on the lookout for opportunities to extend grace to others. I secretly think of this as my Giving Project. It is a way for me to pass on the grace that God and others have shown me. It may take different forms than I experienced, but I am a different person with different gifts to offer. My prayer each day now is "Lord, please give me eyes to see who needs a me-sized blessing." And I almost always mean it. Because I know that there are ways that I can extend grace in exactly the way that someone needs me to. But I have to be paying attention.

I have to have open eyes and an open heart so that I don't miss my chance. I need to be listening for that still small voice—you know the one. It's that highly annoying voice that usually asks you to do something you don't really want to. It whispers quietly enough that you can pretend you don't hear it. And that is a shame, because every time, and I mean *every time* I listen to that voice, I am blessed way beyond any blessing I'm sharing with another. Even if that person didn't know it was me or doesn't respond positively or doesn't say thanks it makes no difference. I followed what I know God wanted me to do and that feels amazing on the inside of me.

I usually try to argue with that voice for awhile, especially if it is telling me to do something super inconvenient. Are you sure, Lord? That struggling single mom looks okay to me. I'm sure she has friends or family that can help her out by watching her baby. Hello, I already have three kids and that would be complete insanity. Wouldn't it be a better use of my time to hang out with my own kids for some "quality time?"

To which that still, small voice answers "Only you can do this for her." It turns out that the voice is right. Even though it is truly the last thing I want to do with any free time I might have, I end up being blessed by watching my kids play with someone else's baby and how they now understand that Mama is helping our friend because people used to watch my babies to help me out. I owe so much that this is the very least I can do.

There is no way I can get close to breaking even in the grace department. We do not do anything to deserve grace, and yet, there it is anyway. This is a great reminder when you are asked to extend grace to family. That's the hardest kind of grace ever! To friends or even strangers, sticking our neck out is sometimes easier than with loved ones. When I am tired because I got up with the baby and I am "working" from home with two of my three little ones underfoot and my husband is golfing and getting some much needed time to himself, it's hard for me to want to show him grace and bless him by giving anything else. Didn't he already get to go golfing? Isn't that enough Lord?

But then there is that stupid little voice that I know is right saying how great it is that I am married to a man who works so hard and is taking some time for himself so he can be a better husband and daddy. Shouldn't I greet him with a sweet smile and hug when he gets home? On top of that, wouldn't it be nice if I had put away all the laundry so he wouldn't have to help with it?

I'm ashamed to admit that I grudgingly whine, "But what about me? I've been working my tushy off all day and I'm tired and since he got to play it's my turn to slack off!" Sigh. Except something funny happens when I go ahead and just do what that voice is telling me to do. It seems to set off a chain-reaction in our house. I give, and then somehow, it all comes back to me. Maybe Mr. Wonderful decides I need a foot rub. Or maybe he gives all the kids a bath to give me a break. Grace is contagious, getting passed around quicker than that stomach virus your kids came home with last flu season. I end up getting blessed ten-fold, and what I did somehow wasn't nearly the sacrifice I thought it would be.

Grace is sacrificial in nature, but you can never out-sacrifice God. I mean, He did send His only son to give his life for us. I don't know anyone that could do that, yet God did. I wonder what would happen if every Christian just in my hometown did one nice thing for someone else every day. What kind of revolution could that start? I know that lives would change. I believe that the effects of that one nice thing would have a ripple effect and go far beyond just my hometown. What if all the Christians in my state did that? Or our nation? What kind of giant grace tsunami would sweep across the country? Only instead of billions of dollars of devastation, we would have immeasurable acts of kindness all around the world. What would that even look like?

What if grace were the hottest new trend? Instead of yet another reality television show or the iPhone2000, what if grace was the new black? Maybe, just maybe, when I start listening to that voice and extending grace to others wherever it's guiding me, some of *those* others will do the same.

Now wouldn't that just be something else?

Part II

Pouring and Savoring

How To Be a Newlywed
Part Deux

Being a newlywed is wonderful. Time alone with just you and your new spouse, discovering how to be a married couple, taking spontaneous trips, walking around stark naked. At least that's how it's supposed to be. Things are a little different when you get remarried and one of you has two kids under the age of six. It gets even more interesting when you get pregnant with a third child immediately after getting married. Newlywed life looks more like this: waking up before the sun because there's a baby crying and there are two pairs of eyes staring at you from three inches away, taking thirty minutes just to get out of the house to go to the grocery store, and walking around in a daze from the lack of sleep.

This new beginning has been a wonderful and interesting ride for me and Mr. Wonderful. Here we are, a newly minted couple in our 30s, still in that barely-able-to-keep-our-hands-off-each-other stage, and there are three little distractions everywhere we go. Thank goodness for early bedtimes! We both adore these children, but three kids make things a little more challenging on the newlywed front.

For instance, recently the kids were napping (or so we thought) and Mr. Wonderful and I decided to grab some much needed alone time. However, we didn't lock the door. You can see where this is going, right? Fortunately we were still mostly clothed as two little boys, one dressed as a pirate and the other carrying a light saber, burst into our bedroom wondering if they could have a snack. It was then that I had the distinct feeling of déjà vu. It was like I was back in high school and didn't want to get caught by my parents making out with my boyfriend on their couch. Only this time, I didn't want my kids to catch me. That's a trip.

That moment won't be going on our parenting highlight reel, but now we are quite vigilant about locking the door. Like any parents, we do the best we can. Mr. Wonderful, from day one of meeting the kids, jumped in wholeheartedly. It has been a beautiful thing to watch these three men in my life create a whole new relationship with a bond totally different from my mama bond. He's the go-to guy when it comes to Wrestle Time, questions about soccer rules, and how to defend yourself against bullies. He's there for them for so much more, too. If a baby needs to be fed or diapered, he's on it. When someone gets a boo-boo, they're just as likely to ask Mr. Wonderful to kiss it as they are to ask me. I love that!

To balance all of our family time, we also try to have enough couple time to nourish our relationship. This is the hard part. As any parent knows, alone time with your spouse is hard to come by. In our short married life, we've already discovered a few things. Early bedtimes for the kids are a must. Not just because little kids need lots of sleep, but because we need time to connect and have a grownup conversation where we get to finish our sentences.

We have also instituted a weekly date night. This is an unbreakable-except-in-emergencies-where-someone's-bleeding-or-vomiting-or-has-a-body-part-hanging-the-wrong-way contract between me and Mr. Wonderful. Nothing short of death or destruction will keep us from eating a meal together and looking each other in the eyes, enjoying each other's company, and reconnecting on an intimate level that's difficult to achieve with kids running around.

I do love that early bedtime! I know as parents we have lots to do before going to bed, but as newlyweds, most of that goes by the wayside. We get our bills paid and there's usually enough food in the fridge and pantry to keep us fed. Everyone *almost* always wears clean underpants. But our house is kind of a mess, there are piles of laundry that need to be put away, and there are usually dishes in the sink. Because at 8:00 on the nose when the kids go to bed, so do we.

We completely shut down the house—lights off, work finished. It probably looks like no one's home. That's because we retire to our room for about three hours of just being together. Our bedroom has become our saving grace in the midst of the chaos. Occasionally, we make our bed and pick up our clothes. We may even take out dirty dishes that have lingered from the evening before. We have a giant, comfy king-size bed with lots of pillows and blankets, and that's our meeting place each night.

That big bed is where Mr. Wonderful and I regroup after a long day. We talk about work or the kids or the funny or bad or serious or wonderful things that happened during our day while we were apart. We snuggle and smooch, watch movies or the shows we DVR-ed. We laugh, we cry, we enjoy the relative silence created within our oasis. We read. We do our daily devotionals and nightly prayers. We do newlywed things. We get much needed rest.

I so look forward to our eight o'clock bed time—I haven't gone to bed this early since third grade! Without it, I don't know how we'd manage. I understand this second trip around the marriage lane that creating intimacy by reconnecting on a daily basis is absolutely essential to a healthy relationship. Carving out time, every day, has been lifted to the very top of my priority list. This baby marriage has the absolute potential to go the distance to be one of those old-couples-still-holding-hands relationships. I want to protect it and nurture it and grow it in every way possible.

The world tells me we won't be newlyweds forever. It says the passion will fade and we'll start taking each other for granted and we only have, at best, a fifty-fifty shot at success. That's so discouraging—until I look at my grandparents. They just celebrated their sixty-fourth wedding anniversary, and I've never seen two people more in love. They're that elderly couple who sits next to each other in a booth, still brimming over with things to talk about after all these years. Grandpa Stanley still teases his bride, flirting with her every chance he gets, opening her car door, buying her special little gifts just because. And Grandma Ginger talks all the time about how she's going out to eat with her boyfriend. They still even have date night.

Every Friday, after all their chores are done, my grandparents get gussied up for each other. They put on their smell-good and Sunday best, and my grandma and grandpa go out on the town for a nice meal and some good conversation. Sometimes they go to the symphony. Sometimes they take a drive. Sometimes they go out with friends. But for as long as I can remember, Friday night has been sacred time between the two of them.

I want something sacred like that for me and Mr. Wonderful; something that will stand the test of time. Though the world bashes relationships and their permanency, I have a shining example of how it can actually work. Watching my grandparents has been like reading a real-life how-to manual in romance and creating your own love story. They've weathered the storms together, letting trauma or disappointment or hard times bind them together instead of tear them apart. They still argue and fuss at times. But through it all, it's obvious that they still enjoy each other's company more than anyone else's. They treat each other like friends and lovers, like they are each other's favorite person in the world.

They are my personal relationship heroes and mentors. This is something I believe every couple just starting out should have. We need examples of how you can still like each other after years and years together. Examples of why you shouldn't give up just because things get hard or go south or are uncomfortable or just downright unbearable. Because it looks like as you get through the tough stuff together, at least as I watch my grandparents, you come out on the other side stronger, better, and in a more rich and wonderful place.

Giving up is the easy choice. Remembering why you married that person in the first place is sometimes hard. Making time for yourselves as a couple, extending grace, learning a lot about forgiveness, and keeping the best things about your partner in the forefront of your mind even when you're supremely irritated seem to be key ingredients in making it work for the long haul.

I remember a moment recently where I was out of my mind cranky with Mr. Wonderful. At his suggestion, we took a time out, and I'll admit, I used the first part of that time just to grind my teeth and wonder what in the world was wrong with that man. After I'd had a few moments to calm down, I started remembering something funny he'd said earlier. And something sweet he'd done for me the day before. And how he kissed my face so gently before he left for work. So right then and there, in the midst of our crankiness at each other, I made a list of reasons why I loved Mr. Wonderful. I had only gotten about three down before I started having good feelings about things again. By the fifth reason, I had forgotten why I was even cranky. At number twenty, I just had to go show Mr. Wonderful the list so we could kiss and make up.

On their sixtieth anniversary, my grandma said to me that she couldn't believe it had been sixty years. For her, it had flown by in the blink of an eye. There were so many good memories that it was hard for her to remember the bad times or the hard times. They were there, but they were just outweighed and overshadowed and put on the back burner by all of the love and generosity and giving each other the benefit of the doubt.

I may be a newlywed again, but something tells me this is all going to go by too fast. Time's a-wastin', and I don't want to lose any of it with Mr. Wonderful. This is my once in a lifetime love. However long we have before the 'til-death-do-us-part business, I want to live every moment possible in love and joy and respect and encouragement. I want to fill it up with the sweetness of memories, so when the rough times hit—and they will again—we have those memories to ride out until we get to the goodness again, the sweetness again.

If you come around my neighborhood at night and people are still outdoors and kids are playing in the street because it's only 8:00 p.m., my house will be dark. It'll be shut down and appear from the outside that no one's home. Because we have three kids that need lots of sleep. And we have a relationship that's only one-sixtieth of the way finished. We're working on creating the sacred within our own relationship, in our own time, in our own way. And when you get the invitation to our sixtieth wedding anniversary party, hosted by all our kids and grandkids and maybe even great-grandkids, you'll understand why.

Awkward

Does anyone else feel like life is just one big series of junior high moments? As if we are all trapped in some smelly, waxed-floor, ego-crushing, insecurity-ridden junior high, complete with cliques and parents who just don't understand and teachers who give too much homework?

At each phase in my life, just when I think I've got it all together I have to start over. Just like I did in junior high. My body is doing strange things that I can't control, and it seems like everyone knows the rules except for me. I oftentimes wonder: what am I doing here?

In junior high, I was a formidable Drama Queen. Those who know me might say nothing has changed but I would like to think that I have at least toned it down a bit. Back then, everything was THE END OF THE WORLD!!!!! My coping mechanisms were still forming: slamming doors, crying, writing, calling my best friends, and procrastinating, some of which—okay, all of which—I still use today.

Most kids start junior high in sixth or seventh grade, so if you are me, you have grown five inches in one summer, gotten boobies, started your period, and developed the distinct feeling that your parents are complete morons. And holy insecurities, Batman! Any one of these things could sideline a person, but all of them together just made me a walking time bomb. It didn't take much to set me off. My Little Brother didn't know how to knock. That was enough to make me start yelling all the bad things I could think of. "You're stupid! Mom and Dad don't love you and you smell like a monkey!" Whenever my parents tried to—heaven forbid—tell me what to do, I could go from calm to screechy hysteria in dot three seconds.

Navigating the world as a junior higher, where you don't ever really know what to say, do, or wear in any given situation seems to be the theme of my life. You barely survive your first few painful years of junior high. Then you get to be at the top of the pile where you pretend to rule all, everyone knows you, and you have a slight understanding what is expected of you both behaviorally and scholastically. Then suddenly, after that awkward, yet glorious year as reigning Top Dog, you are thrust down to the bottom rung again when you start high school. Rinse and repeat with college and your first job out of college and getting married and becoming a parent and getting a divorce and getting remarried. Does it ever end? Does this feeling of not knowing what I am doing a good ninety percent of the time actually ever go away?

Sadly, though I have gotten rid of most of my junior high insecurities, I am occasionally now plagued by a whole new set of grownup ones. Will the other moms like me? Am I doing a good job as a parent? How does that Super-Mom seem to do it all and where can I take lessons? And the little things still set me off. I can't fit into my pre-pregnancy pants! I don't know what I want to do for the rest of my life! Why can't this child sleep in her own bed?

In junior high, my arch nemesis was a girl named Julie who was a year older than me. I was so insignificant she probably didn't even realize she was my arch nemesis. We all know someone like her. She was the girl with the perfectly coiffed hair despite that gale-force Oklahoma wind, she always dated the cutest boy in school, and she was surrounded by her ever-adoring drones willing to do her bidding. She set the bar high in both sports and fashion. While the rest of us were just trying to keep food out of our braces or grow out a bad perm or survive wearing tight white basketball shorts at home games, she was walking around ruling the school looking like a model from the newest Def Leppard video. Complete with wind machine hair.

Now, my grown up arch nemesis is Super-Mom. She probably doesn't even know she is on my list either. I watch her and it just makes me tired. She always has it together somehow. She is on duty 24/7 and would never snicker at the word "duty." Her perfect children always arrive at events well-behaved and stain-free, while my brood arrives in a tangle of noise and chaos and unmatched clothing. Occasionally, one of them has even gone commando. My three-year-old forgets to wear underpants. A lot.

Super-Mom looks immaculate, and her doctor-perfected bosoms look amazing in a swimsuit at the neighborhood pool whereas I am still rocking some post-pregnancy extra baggage. She lives in the biggest, most beautifully decorated house in the neighborhood and she drives the newest car. She always looks like she just stepped out of a very pricey clothing catalogue.

Our car has 447,000 miles on it, our house just got struck by lightning so everything is still on the fritz, and I am still learning how to juggle three kids and a job. And how to find time to take a shower most days. And how to get spit-up out of my dress clothes on the way to a meeting I am late for.

Some days it is overwhelming watching Super-Mom's perfection. And just like in junior high, I cannot help but compare myself. On my good days, I realize that this is a ridiculous concept. There is no reason to compare myself to anyone. I am the only one living this life. But on my worst days, I feel like a freak show carnival act, minus the cool tattoos and the horns growing out of my head. She makes it all look so easy, and she is just so darn perfect, at least from my vantage point. Maybe she is lonely or sad or has insecurities too. I doubt it, but I concede it is possible.

I know the lesson here is that I need to be paying more attention to the good stuff going on in my own life. I should be grateful instead of weirdly stalking this mom in my hood that seems to have it all. On some days, in some ways, I have it mostly together. I manage to know where all of my children are about ninety-five percent of the time. My house, though not immaculate, is a work in progress. I am learning to deal with my cobwebby corners and dirty floors bit by bit. I am working on getting my pre-pregnancy body back by being in the gym at least five days a week. I am trying to do my best at my actual job. I'm also working on being brave enough to write words down, turn them into a book, and then ask people to read it.

Maybe I don't have the hang of this parenting thing yet, but I do have three healthy and happy kids. Maybe all of the junior high moments that keep happening over and over are just changes that we all go through in our lives. Maybe the only way for me to get off that hamster wheel of insecurities is to actively look for and count all of my blessings. And stop worrying about how others are doing their lives and focus on how I do mine.

Then maybe I can move past junior high. At least for a little while.

The Long Way Home

Every person considering marriage should be required by law to take a road trip with their potential spouse. I'm convinced if your relationship can survive the open road, it can probably survive just about anything.

Road trips can be invigorating. There's just something about hitting the open road, seeing things you have never seen before, and watching your mate sleep in uncomfortable positions while drool runs off his or her face. On one of my early vacations with Mr. Wonderful, I discovered something interesting: road trips are a true test of a relationship. What will you talk about for twenty-four straight hours of driving? Will you still be speaking to each other when you reach your destination after being confined to a very small space? Will there be enough rest stops?

When Mr. Wonderful excitedly told me he got to go on an incentive trip he won for being so awesome at his job, I was thrilled. When he told me that if we drove I would get to go for free, I was ecstatic! I *love* free stuff! Then he told me where we were driving. Reno. As in, Nevada. For those of you who are geographically challenged like I am, let me break it down for you. Oklahoma is the state with the panhandle sticking out its left top side and it's smack dab in the middle of the country. And Reno, to my surprise when I looked on a map, is practically in California. That would be nearly 1,700 miles of driving. One way! When I broke that down into the amount of rest stops that would be required for me to make the trip I was a little scared. Would we ever make it there, or would my tiny bladder make me rue the day?

I had some interesting experiences with road trips as a kid. My parents were teachers, so we would usually just take off every summer for a couple of weeks. By the time I was in high school, I had been to something like thirty-five states. I had seen every Civil War battlefield and statue of an important person and probably even the world's largest ball of twine. My parents—and you can question their sanity after I tell you this—had even driven us to Canada. As in, the country with the maple leaf and mispronunciation of certain words. How aboot that?

Looking back, I'm sure that I was just as bad at road trips as I am now. Between the TBS (Teeny Bladder Syndrome) and the car sickness, I was a hoot and half on any car trip. My dad was the master trip planner. Carefully mapping out mileage and rest stops and the best places to stay the night, he was meticulous. He's a point-A-to-point-B-as-quickly-as-possible kind of guy. Travelling with me most surely tested his patience.

Mr. Wonderful suggested the drive would be a chance to finish all those conversations we never get around to since we are outnumbered by small children. I agreed, despite my flashbacks to my road-tripping childhood. Maybe this would be fun. A great way to reconnect. A vacation for two in the midst of our daily chaos. Six whole days together. Constantly. What could possibly go wrong?

Something you should know about Mr. Wonderful and me: we are a great team. No two people were ever so prepared for a road trip. My dad would have been proud. The car was washed and vacuumed, there was an ice chest full of snacks and drinks, and we had so much to catch up on after an especially busy month for the both of us. I was really starting to come around—this was going to be the best trip ever!

We set out, much like I imagined the Pilgrims did, or Lewis and Clark. Only we had GPS and the internet on our phone and there would be plenty of rest stops. We laughed and talked and I felt us bonding and reconnecting in a way that we had not been able to for awhile. Sometimes it just takes some deliberate time spent together with no interruptions to get that done. We talked, hit a rest stop, ate, hit another rest stop, made lists of "Places We'd Like to Go," and found yet another rest stop. It really was not as bad as I had anticipated, because I had my partner, my best friend, my lover and confidant right there in the car with me.

And then, of course, we hit road construction. The speed limit reduction always starts miles before the actual road work, and this was no exception. Down to one lane. Puttering behind some sweet old lady who thought the fifty-five miles per hour posted was much too fast so forty-five would be more appropriate. So exasperating! We were making such good time and now this.

A long road trip can force stuff to come up. All kinds of business will rise to the surface like cream. Or in some cases, pond scum. Sometimes it's ugly. Maybe there are things one doesn't want to say and the other doesn't want to hear. I guarantee, if you stay in a car long enough, this small cramped moving confessional will force conversations you never wanted to have. Ones that you did not even know you *needed* to have.

You will take detours and experience relationship road construction. You may fight, you may cry, you may even wish you could go back to mile 237 before you started asking questions and winding down a road that doesn't appear on any map. At this point in your relationship, the road construction phase where you are going forty-five in a fifty-five and there doesn't seem to be any end in sight, one of two things will happen. You will either make your way through it. Or someone will get left by the side of the road.

Being stuck at this place in the journey is no fun. Besides being out of good snacks by then and having my bladder screaming at me yet again, I was in a car with someone that suddenly looked less familiar to me. Who was this person? What in God's creation were we doing in a car eight hours from home and sixteen from our destination? It was too far to turn around and go back home. Should we push through? Could we?

After a brief meltdown on both of our parts, we decided to pray. To seek guidance. To keep us from killing each other. There was something about that raw reaching out to the same God by us both that took our relationship to a new place. Oh, we were not done with our discussions by far. In fact, we had a lot of rough, unpaved road still to cover. But we seemed to be reminded of our place in each other's hearts. And that we were not alone. That knowledge helped change the tone of everything. We remembered that we had promised to be gentle with one another, and even though neither one of us wanted to be in the midst of this particular discussion, we were committed. To each other. To our relationship. To God our Father.

We started really talking in earnest, asking what the other needed. We were going to somehow get through this near-disaster and no one was going to be unceremoniously kicked out of the car or left at the next gas station to find their way home alone. We were in the desert, but we were not without our oasis.

As we talked and cried and thought and forgave and remembered, we seemed to be climbing out of the broken down place where we had gotten stuck. We realized that we have great power—both the power to hurt each other deeply and the power to love each other better than we have ever been loved. The power to help heal each other's wounds, both seen and unseen. There were times when that road trip turned dark, but it may have been one of the best things we could have done for ourselves.

Being in a relationship with another human being is fraught with peril. By giving him the key to my heart, I am also giving Mr. Wonderful access to every tool he needs to hurt me. He knows me better than anyone, better than I have ever let anyone know me. And that gives him the knowledge of what would hurt me the most. It is up to him to use his knowledge for good, not evil, and the same goes for me.

On our road trip, God became the oil to our relationship. He filled in all the gaps, held us together, kept things moving forward and running better. Without Him, I am pretty sure one of us would have been hitch-hiking home.

That road trip was so much more than I ever expected. I learned so much about a man I thought I knew everything about. I found out how good he can be in the midst of the bumps in the road. I realized how great he is at taking care of me and my tiny bladder. We did a lot of talking, and we did a lot of laughing and loving too. I am so grateful for my chance at reconnecting with the man I love. What a surprising gift it was to be stuck in a car for twenty-four hours. The stay at the resort was beautiful and the food was amazing, but my favorite part of our trip was in the car.

The fact that we still liked each other at the end of it was, in its own way, a road trip miracle. I think I'm even ready for our next one.

Vegas, anyone?

Lake People

Lake People are a different breed of folks. They are no better or worse than any others, just different. At the lake, there's no rush. There is no hurry, and no particular place you have to be by any certain time. No one wears a watch, and there is this magnificent freedom in eating when you get hungry, sleeping when you're tired, and playing when you're not doing anything else. It is almost like being a child again. You do things the way God intended. I have always wanted to be Lake People, and last summer, my dream finally came to fruition.

As brand new baby Lake People, Mr. Wonderful and I had some rules to learn about lake livin'. Mainly that there are no rules. There is no time. No stress allowed. And talk about work or mortgages or bad bosses or that stupid guy who cut you off when you were already running late just doesn't happen. No whining or fighting or back-stabbing. Only good times, good friends, great food, and perfect margaritas. Can't you see why we'd want to be part of this club?

When I was a kid, some of my fondest memories involved the lake. It was a dirty, disgusting lake, but it was twenty minutes from my house and it was where our youth group sponsors had their boat. It was where I learned to water ski, make s'mores, and leave all my cares behind. It's where my friends and I grew up, learned a little about life, and made memories together. It was the destination of choice after a hot summer day of working as a waitress at my small town greasy spoon café. I would load up my car with bags of Cheetos, a cooler full of drinks, and my best friends cranking up the tunes.

When Mr. Wonderful and I met, I had been on hiatus from the lake for some time. Somehow, my life had gotten in the way of my lake time. I no longer hung out with people who loved the lake like I did. I worked too hard, had little kids and too many excuses to be a bona fide Lake Person. Mr. Wonderful and I quickly discovered that we both loved being around the water and taking road trips together. Soon, we had all these friends who seemed to be Lake People. We dreamed of ways we could become Lake People too. It seemed like forever, but finally, last summer we were able to make it work and took our first step toward official lake life: we bought a travel trailer.

For the uninitiated, this is the crucial first step to becoming Lake People. Yes, you could buy a boat first, but then you're stuck hauling it back and forth each day of the weekend. Our thinking led us to the conclusion that it was a moral imperative to buy our redneck "lakehouse" first. This way we always have our home away from home with us. We're not tied to one lake, we can travel year-round, and we have friends with boats. What more do we need?

Our first weekend in our travel trailer was glorious, despite record-breaking temperatures. It was a heated 108 degrees! It was hot, but as I told Mr. Wonderful, the only way I'll go camping is if I have an air conditioner and a restroom. I freely admit I'm that kind of girl. You will not catch me camping in a tent unless it's with my small children in my living room, and even then, I'm pretty likely to bail by midnight and sleep in my own bed.

After an entire summer of spending every moment at the lake that we could, I dare you to ask our kids what's the rule at the lake. Their response is sure to be, "There's no time at the lake!" This concept really threw Big Brother for awhile at the beginning of our lake initiation period. He just didn't understand that you don't always have to know what time it is to be having fun. This is the kid who likes things Just So. If they are not, he gets all out of sorts. He's a perfectionist, he loves knowing that there is a certain schedule or order to his life, and he enjoys knowing what is coming next.

At first, Lake Living, or Livin', was hard for Big Brother. Slowly, though, as the summer wore on, he didn't seem to mind that all the kids' clothes were kept in a big pile of shorts and T-shirts, so just pick what you want to wear today. It doesn't matter if it matches. Pretty soon, we noticed he stopped asking what we were going to do next or what time we thought it was. He was having entirely too much fun to care about such mundane things.

He and Little Brother were racing around our "neighborhood" with their own set of Lake Friends. They would decide that it was time to eat, so Big Brother would make a couple of sandwiches or get snacks and juice boxes—he knew where everything was and that it was okay to just help himself. If the boys were sleepy, they would lie down on their bunk beds, maybe watch a movie, and then pass out from the sheer exhaustion of having too much fun all day long. Our boys watched the stars come out at night, something that we don't get to do in the city. We heard crickets and boats being docked and people laughing and someone several trailers over playing guitar.

We woke up, sometimes with the sun. We drank coffee outside under our little awning over our front porch. We ate scrambled eggs and fish and sandwiches and Oreos and fresh fruit. We stayed out on the water all day, swimming or napping. The boys ran and skipped and played in the sand and made friends with other kids and swam. They got to be kids. We got to be grownups without a care in the world on those lake weekends.

I love being Lake People. I love not having to look at a clock or a computer screen. It's great to have a little community of like-minded people who enjoy swimming or boating in the lake during the day, cooking out for dinner, and then sipping cool drinks by the light of the actual moon. We told stories, laughed and played cards or watched movies at night. If I make this life sound idyllic, believe me—it is. We will be getting away every chance we get, because it makes us be the kind of people I think God really likes: grateful.

Even Jesus was Lake People. A lot of stories about him involve him and his disciples gathered around a body of water. His people were fishermen. He preached at the lake. For Peter's sake, he even walked on water. It makes me smile to think that Jesus really understood the idea of Lake Livin'. Time slows down, you connect with friends old and new, you break bread together.

As Lake People, we are able to focus on the things that really matter: making memories with our kids, enjoying God's beautiful outdoors, slowing down. I joke, but there was a kernel of truth to the fact that I told everyone my summer address is lakeside.

Having our travel trailer is such a blessing. There's only so much you can put in there, so you have to be very particular. No clutter and no unnecessary items allowed inside. There isn't room for mental clutter at the lake either. You can't obsess about work or people who make you angry or sad or frustrated. You can't fight with your spouse or your kids for long—you'd miss out on too much fun.

There's no time at the lake, so there's no time to waste or get behind or catch up to. It is what it is, and if you spend lots of time at the lake, I guarantee your priorities will change. I'm living a richer, fuller life because I'm appreciating my blessings in a whole new way. I'm remembering what it's like to enjoy spending time with my kids, not just march them from one activity to the next. I'm reconnecting with Mr. Wonderful because we don't have the distractions and To Do Lists and junk of life weighing us down. We just have our family and the water and some cooking out. Every day is a new adventure or memory waiting to happen, and it makes me so grateful to finally be Lake People.

Expectations

I usually wake up in the morning expecting my day to be fairly sunny, despite the weather outside. I don't love mornings, but once I get my coffee groove on and I've started my day before the kids wake up so I've had time to be productive, I'm usually feeling my oats.

Unless I've had a rough night. Then I'm a bear and everyone around me better stay out of the way of my claws and my tongue. You will rue the day you tried to talk to me when I was in a morning funk. I can be ill-tempered and frankly kind of nasty—not myself at all.

This morning was a morning like that. Sometimes it's not easy sharing a bed with a man built like an NFL linebacker. I love it because I'm a snuggler and Mr. Wonderful is always warm and I feel extremely safe when he's near. I know the bad guys would have to go through him before they'd get to me. Trust me, he would be a formidable opponent.

Which brings me to my next point: he's a formidable opponent in the sleep wars. Let's just say I'm always on the losing end when his powerful arm comes swinging across the bed as he changes positions in his sleep. His wingspan is 6'6" so even a king-sized bed can't protect me from that mighty hand smacking me in the head. It's completely accidental but try telling me that in the middle of the night when I'm awakened from a deep and beautiful sleep by seemingly running into a brick wall. I'm a bear now, and poor Mr. Wonderful awoke to his Bride of Frankenstein this morning. No wonder he left for work so early.

Now that he's gone, I'm feeling bad about how I helped start his day off. He has come to expect smiles and lovey-doveyness in the morning, and I filled his few minutes before he left (super early to work hard for his family, by the way) with my extreme form of crankiness. Even though I apologized before he left, I'm still feeling like I may have given him a case of the Monday blues. That's a terrible thought.

Expectations can be good or bad. They can set the tone for your day. Expect something awesome to happen, and it probably will. Expect something awful, and you'll probably get that as well. Henry Ford said, "Whether you think you can or think you can't, you're right." What goes on in our mind and comes out of our mouths is important. We are all expecting different things during our days: reports from the doctor, promotions, babies, checks in the mail, friends to drop by. Some of them will be good and some won't. That's where our expectations come in.

Expecting things to go well sets up all of the good that is headed your way. It's like a welcome mat near the door that helps usher the amazing in. But it is seriously hard to keep that welcome mat swept off when you've been up with a child three times in the middle of the night or you're worried about how you're going to pay your bills or if your job is safe or if your insurance will pay for that test you need. I get this.

When I was a single mom, my worries felt so heavy that I sometimes felt crushed under their sheer weight.

I didn't have anyone else to help me with them. I had to worry about whether I could pay my mortgage by myself or whether I would be able to afford child care that was inexpensive but not scary. Or if my sweet babies were going to survive divorce.

My worries sometimes overwhelmed me because I tried to deal with them all by myself. Being a single mom, I thought I had to at first. That season of my life taught me to lean on God. I mean really *lean*. Rely on him. Trust him like never before. He was going to be my provider and my rock and my shelter, if only I would ease up on this trying-to-do-it-alone thing and let him help. When I stopped expecting that I would have to do everything myself, I was able to see that God was already there, waiting to help me had my stubborn self just let go of the expectation that I was alone.

When you get married or remarried, you probably have certain expectations as well. People think that their marriage will be this way or that. When it's not it's usually because we forgot to inform the other party of our expectations or we didn't talk about who would take care of the money or the dishes or how we would handle discipline or whether we would even have children or where we would store all our extra baggage from previous relationships. We get disappointed or frustrated. Sometimes we just give up.

Relationships are hard. They take work and tending to and talking about, hopefully with the other person involved. Expectations can make or break relationships. Expecting your spouse to read your mind is probably not a good thing. Expecting to grow old with someone and taking the word divorce right out of the equation probably is.

Family relationships are no different. In fact, they are probably the trickiest. These are people who changed your diapers and saw you through the awkwardness and bad hair choices of puberty. Maybe they even helped you pay for college. Talk about expectations! You *will* grow up to be a productive citizen and you *will* move out of this house and support yourself. Or maybe the expectation is more along the lines of they knew you when so they won't stray from that old image of you in their minds. Did you used to be a loser or a complete screw up? Good luck changing their expectations of you.

I admit, I even have expectations of total strangers. I expect to be able to win them over with a little chit chat about things I've noticed about them while standing in line or my sweet smile or these cute kids I bring with me nearly everywhere. I expect that they will be, at the very least, courteous. Sadly, a lot of times my expectations are too high. I have to remind myself that maybe that person just had a fight with a loved one or found out she's being evicted or he wasn't raised with much kindness so he doesn't know he's supposed to be kind in return.

It's taken me a long time to not take it personally when someone is rude. I have to take a step back and remind myself that everyone has a bad day and I should give them the benefit of the doubt. I used to not only take it personally, but I would stew over every affront by anyone I met. I would mutter things under my breath about how sad it is that we live in a country where men no longer open the door for a woman struggling to get her children inside out of the inclement weather. Or how I wished that person that just cut me off in traffic would be forced to take their driver's test again because obviously they've forgotten a few things.

Now, for the most part, I try to take a deep breath and wish them well. It may sound ridiculous, but sometimes I even say, "God bless you." They don't hear me, but I do, and if the kids are with me, they do too. This is a much better example than when I use my "driving words." Especially when I have little parrots in my backseat who will mimic me perfectly, right down to my tone and shaking fist.

Sometimes we can't choose our circumstances, but we can always choose our responses to them. Things in life inevitably break down, fall apart, and come undone. This is just part of being alive. Dishwashers and hearts break. People leave. Friends disappoint. Sickness comes around. There's no magic cure for avoiding bad things happening. When that stuff happens, though, is when we are presented with an opportunity for growth.

Ahhhh! Growing—it's so painful. Personally, I like living a stunted life most of the time, trying to ignore what God is teaching me as he's walking me through the hard parts. But it turns out, staying stunted ends up being almost as painful as the actual place of pain. The growth part may be hard, but after I go through it, I'm always glad to be at the new place. Expectations during hard times can certainly make those hard times go either way. You can expect that there will be an end and that God is right there with you. Or you can expect that things are always going to be rotten. And they probably will be.

It's hard to expect good things in the middle of the bad. You can't see the end yet and you long for the beginning because at least it wasn't the middle. Yet if you have expectations every morning when you wake up that today might be the day—the day you sell your house, the day your loved one kicks an addiction, the day you reconnect with your spouse—you set up the possibility of something better. Some *place* better.

We can't control people around us or the places that we sometimes end up because of others. Believe me, I've tried. But we can expect good things around every corner, even if we haven't seen a good thing for a long time coming. God is moving and shaking and working in ways we can't see or understand, so this is possible. Growth is the intersection where hope and faith collide, where things get really real. It's the true testing grounds of a Christian. Expect good things or great things or amazing things just because. They. Are. Coming.

I guess now would probably be a good time for me to call Mr. Wonderful and tell him how much I appreciate him and how I'm expecting great stuff to happen for the both of us today. No matter what things look like at the end of this day, I will at least have poured some words of kindness and goodness into him.

When it comes to expectations, that can make all the difference.

Relationship Tchotchkes

I'm not a scrapbooker. People who know me are shocked when I say this because I usually embrace all things artsy. It's kind of amazing to me as well—how am I neglecting an entire genre that fills up a rather large corner of my favorite crafts store? I'm completely capable; I just have no interest in it. I haven't even completed a baby book since the one I did in fourth grade for my Cabbage Patch doll. Instead, I'm a tchotchke saver. A memory compiler. Okay, a pack rat.

I love to keep things from specific memories or trips or moments. After Mr. Wonderful and I got married, we went on our Dream Honeymoon—it was so incredible it has to be capitalized. We basically Craigslist-ed our way into this trip to Mexico, and we were so excited to travel together. We splurged and upgraded to first-class seats at the last minute, and got to do things like have champagne at 8:00 in the morning and go in the first-class only President's Club at the airport—I didn't even know such a thing existed. I would tell you all about it, but I am sworn to secrecy to keep all the riff-raff out.

Our postcard resort sat right next to the ocean with the most gorgeous turquoise water and sugary sand. When we checked in, this nice young man behind the check-in desk gave us an upgrade to the best room—excuse me, the best house—on the resort grounds because we were new-lyweds and because God was smiling down on us that day. As we unpacked in our casita with the view of the beach just beyond the pool that was literally off our back patio, we marveled at our trip. There were restaurants and beach lounging beds and a gym that we visited twice a day to work off the copious amounts of food and beverage we were consuming. There was room service and housekeepers who would arrange our towels in little animal shapes and a swim up bar. We had an outdoor shower and a Jacuzzi tub, and we could have our choice of catching some rays either on our back patio while dipping our feet into the swim-ming pool or on the beach, where we could dip our feet into the ocean.

We made "resort friends." These are the people that are staying right around you so you keep running into them while you're there. Ours was a young couple from Missouri who had been married for awhile and were taking a vaca-tion from their kids. Laughing, I told them that we were taking our Honeymoon to get away from our kids. They were so fun! We told stories and laughed and got pruny by staying too long at the swim up bar and drinking all the yummy concoctions the bartender dreamed up.

The first day we were there, Mr. Wonderful made the mistake of asking the bartender what time it was. Strangely, the bartender didn't answer right away. He just turned his back and went about his task of making drinks. I could tell Mr. Wonderful had had just about enough of being ignored. And then the bartender placed shots of tequila on the bar, one for everyone in the pool at that time and said with a completely straight face, "It's Tequila Time." Even the bartender was full of life and laughter, and he did a great job of entertaining his crowd.

Mr. Wonderful and I dreamed about how we could leave it all behind, pick up the kids, and somehow move to this paradise. With the Mexican drug cartel to contend with and the extreme poverty all around, we knew it wasn't all paradise. But it felt good to fantasize about leaving all our responsibilities and having jobs like making arts and crafts to sell to tourist (me) and working security (him).

This was a place with no time, pristine beaches, amazing food, flowers, and ocean views and wide open blue skies. I have never been anyplace so beautiful. The last day, I scooped up some sand from the beach, put it in a water bottle, and packed it in my suitcase. I found out from the kind gentleman at the border who checks your passports and asks if you have anything to declare that you're really not supposed to do this. Apparently there are microbes or some such thing that can do bad things. Frankly, I didn't listen to anything past "You're really not supposed to do that." He did let me keep my bottle of sand though.

I wanted that bottle to remind me of our trip of a lifetime. Our perfect little honeymoon. I wanted to be able to show my kids the sand from a beach that wasn't the lake we visit nearly every weekend in the summer. I needed this reminder, this tchotchke of a time when we were a newly minted "official" couple and things were shiny and unspoiled by time or circumstance or words we couldn't take back. That way when the hard times come and we are in the middle of the muck, I'll have that sand—that perfect white sand—to take me away to one of our best places so far.

Mr. Wonderful and I joke about jumping into year ten of our marriage. With two kids to start the marriage and then suddenly getting pregnant to add a third, we didn't begin our newlywed year like most people do. In our first year, we merged two entire households, sold a house, traded in a couple of cars, had a baby, and bought a travel trailer. These are things couples do who have been married a lot longer than we have been. Still, in actual time, our marriage is young, so there will be lots of other tchotchkes from lots of other trips and experiences.

I collect everything about our relationship. Mr. Wonderful is a great writer of notes, and I have saved every last one of them. My stack is growing tall, and it's probably time to get a bigger box, but I hope that continues throughout our marriage. Someday, I'll be old. Notice I didn't say gray. I have a deal with Laura, my friend and hair guru, that she is not supposed to tell me when I am gray. She's just supposed to cover it up. I may already be gray and just not know it. Come to think of it, with all these kids running around, I probably am.

I hope that when we have stood the test of time and weathered storms together and maybe we're downsizing our house since the kids are all grown and gone, my daughter will be helping me pack up things, and she will see the boxes. She will have an idea of the weight that love letters and tchotchkes and trinkets can have in a life. She will see that Mr. Wonderful has loved me through changing waistlines and wrinkles and mortgages and medical procedures and grandchildren and dream vacations. She will hopefully take away from those stacks of stuff that the love God gives us in a spouse is one that is like no other, one that can only be experienced spread over a lifetime together, however long that lifetime will be.

I hope all of our kids will look at our relationship, and maybe sometimes all of the relationship tchotchkes I have saved, and know that it is possible to love someone with all your heart for a lifetime. Even through the ups and downs, even through triumph or tragedy, love and hard work and a shared faith and absolute commitment to your partner will prevail. I want to give them a good example so they know what to look for in a partner for themselves. I hope they will see how I have treasured my relationship with Mr. Wonderful all those years.

When our kids go through my boxes of tchotchkes, they will find love letters, hospital bracelets, pictures they drew, art projects they made me, adoption brochures, funny things they said that I just had to write down, trinkets from family vacations or weekends at the lake. But they will be seeing more than just random items from my life—they will be seeing my memories as I lived them. It is my dream that they will know how much I treasure my life with all of them by divining it from the relationship tchotchkes that I have saved throughout the years.

Part III

Tiny Bubbles

Oscar the Wonder Dog

If you're not a dog person, you may not get this. I mean a keep-doggie-biscuits-in-your-car-and-buy-sweaters-with-your-family-crest-on-it kind of dog person. Okay, I haven't actually bought Oscar the Wonder Dog a sweater, but it's more because he's barrel-chested and hard to fit than any aversion to doggy clothes on my part.

As of this writing, Oscar is at least fifteen years old. I've learned a lot from this dog. To non-dog people, he may appear to be a mere dog. To me, he's been so much more. You know sometimes you run across a man and you just know that he's a man's man? Well, if all Oscar's doggy friends were sitting around in the dog park barking to each other about Oscar, they'd describe him as a dog's dog. He loves to bark and sniff dog butts with the best of them. He's stinky, and his toots smell like poorly recycled dog food. The older he gets, the more foibles he seems to have: scratching incessantly, only eating his dog food if it's on the floor instead of a bowl, and—I hesitate to tell you this because I don't want you to think less of him—eating dog poop.

He also dreams in his sleep. I love to imagine he's dreaming about chasing the mail man. When he's in the middle of a good, deep sleep, his paws start moving like they did when he was a young pup. He does this muted barking thing, like he's warning that mail carrier to just back the truck up.

This dog has been my constant companion for the last decade and a half. He was a scrawny little stray when I found him. I took one look at him and fell in love. Then I took him to the vet, got him his shots, and named him Oscar. We've been inseparable ever since. Through thick and thin—I'm talking about both our weights here—heartbreak and sorrow, the adoptions of my two boys, the birth of my daughter, the funerals of my grandpa and grandma, late night law school study sessions, not knowing what I wanted to be when I grew up, seven moves, the demise of my marriage, birthdays, binges, my remarriage to Mr. Wonderful, long walks, lazy Sunday afternoon naps, belly rubs, the daily ritual of barking at the mail carrier, and all the other ups and downs of the last decade plus.

He has been my ever-constant, ever-faithful Oscar. He has never wavered in his devotion. Oscar has a strong commitment to being the best dog he can be. He never fails to greet me at the door, tail wagging his excitement. It's like he's saying "I'm SO happy you're home—we have so much to talk about while you scratch my belly!" He seems to have a sixth sense about when I'm sad, choosing to quietly sit by my side, watching me with worried eyes if I'm crying. He knows when I'm crazy upset, choosing to lend his support from afar by staying out of my way.

He fully understands what it's like to live joyfully. He's great about showing gratitude, even for the little things. When he gets a treat or tummy rub, it's like he won the lottery. Oscar also understands that his role at our house is multi-faceted: not only is he the greeter of everyone who walks in the door, but he's also the protector, a role he took to heart especially once there were children in the house.

Big Brother was five months old when he was adopted. The first few days at home were a daze—there was suddenly a new baby that I was getting to know while studying for law school finals while figuring out what this mom thing really meant. Between diapers and feedings and case studies and no sleep, Oscar was there.

In the beginning, he didn't know what to do about the little bundle that made awful noises at all times of the night and day. At the first cry, Oscar would come and get me, wherever I was, begging me with his eyes to please make it stop. He would pace back and forth from where I was to where the baby was and back again until I was at last reunited with the noisy little thing. After all was calm again, he would circle around his spot once, flop on the floor with a sigh, and instantly fall into an exhausted sleep. His life was suddenly much more complicated!

As each baby has come home, Oscar has left his post in our room to sleep in the nursery or just outside it. I still wake up to find Oscar sleeping on the kids' side of the house protecting all the kids from harm.

Oscar is truly a Wonder Dog—he's had several lives up to this point. He almost got run over by a mail truck when he dashed out of an open door. He's had a run-in with the law, aka Animal Control, after he bit an actual mail man. I know, so cliché. In Oscar's defense, the guy was on our property and Oscar thought he was attacking eight-month-old Big Brother who was sitting in the doorway. He's eaten a tub of butter, half a package of Oreos, a loaf of bread, his weight in dog poop, and I'm pretty sure a couple of dead birds. I should probably get his cholesterol checked.

Oscar is so thoughtful; he even brought me a gift once. One early morning before I could even get my contacts in, Oscar was signaling his increasing need to go outside. At this house, there wasn't a fence around the yard, so I would just accompany him outside and wait until he was finished. This particular morning I noticed he appeared to be digging around one area more than usual, but I couldn't really see what was going on. When I called him in, he came trotting up to me, proud as he could be, with what appeared to be a wiggly rock in his mouth.

Upon further and unfortunately closer inspection, I realized it was a mouse. And it was alive. Oscar is part retriever, so he was gently holding the squirming vermin in his mouth, presenting it to me as if it were made of fourteen-karat gold. I screamed and began to run around the house to get away from the mouse. Oscar thought we were playing a fun new game called "Chase Mama with the Mouse!" I ran inside and slammed the door in his face. Let's just say that I paid dearly for my behavior. He wouldn't look at me the rest of the day as punishment for rejecting his "gift."

This dog knows the meaning of unconditional love. He still shows me his special tail-wagging brand of love even if I've yelled at him for eating part of a chocolate cake that I had the unfortunate lapse in judgment to leave near the edge of the counter. He loves me even when I forget to fill his water bowl or we take too long in letting him outside or we just forget about him because we're too entrenched in the business—the busyness—of life. Is it any coincidence that God is dog spelled backwards?

Sweet, sweet Oscar. Thanks for sticking with me old buddy. You truly are a Wonder Dog.

In God We Trust

My oldest, Big Brother, recently informed me that the phrase "IN GOD WE TRUST" is on money and that it is our national motto. I knew that. Well, after a little research on *Wikipedia*, I knew that. Apparently, "IN GOD WE TRUST" has been circulating on our money in some form or fashion since the Civil War. In 1956, Congress officially adopted it as our motto, and in 2011, it was reaffirmed as such.

Isn't it great to live in a country with a motto? Makes us sound so together. I still think we must live in the grandest country in the world. I have an automatic coffee pot that magically (when I remember to put the coffee grounds and water in the night before) has coffee waiting for me at 5:00 a.m. I also live in a house with an automatic garage door opener, a backyard a little bigger than a handkerchief, and I have a bathtub with jets in it. Am I living in the lap of luxury or what? Only in America, the land of the free and the home of the brave, can one experience so much amazing technology and appliancery to make life better.

People, including my husband, have fought for my right to live, work, play, and utilize automation in this Land of Possibility. "IN GOD WE TRUST" is on our money so we must be the best—we have God on our side. Even if not all of us believe that and the ones who do are quiet about it, I think God is still pulling for us. Despite the economy, the awful statistics about practically everything, and the threat that the Dow might fall again today we still live in an incredible country. Sidebar: does anyone actually know what the Dow is? It's hard to believe it though, when the news is constantly reminding us that gas is so expensive it costs your firstborn just to drive across town. There is noise about how the unemployment rate is horrible and there are no jobs anywhere and everyone is looking. At least that is the news I hear.

I know people who don't currently have a job. And it is stressful and hard and they are worried about how they are going to take care of their kids and make their mortgage payment and go to the eye doctor when their insurance benefits run out. But the ones I know are trying to trust God that he will provide. They are doing their part to find work, be frugal, and reach out for help when they need it.

I actually know more people *with* jobs than without. I realize this can be regional, and us Okies have certainly been through our share of hard times. Those of us who are working may not have our dream jobs of being a rock star or an actress—or in my specific case—an Olympic athlete or circus performer; I can't decide. But we do have ways to put food on our table and pay for a place to live and buy our kids' winter coats and try to help out those who have fallen on harder times.

News about this particular time in our country just sounds like static to me now. It's all white noise and its only purpose is to frighten and panic and sell newspapers or advertisements. It's possible that all that negativity is keeping people from remembering what a great place we

live in. We are better than this—we are in America, people! We can say whatever we want, no matter how idiotic
it makes us sound. We can pierce things or dye our hair or
have as many tattoos as we feel like. We can spend more
than we make or take out mortgages on homes we should
never have taken out mortgages on in the first place. We
can criticize the government *and* the stupid people we
voted in. We have the much taken-for-granted right to
vote. On everything, including who will be president, the
next American Idol, or if anyone's actually got talent. We
have Disneyworld and the Grand Canyon and Hawaii and
Redwoods and the Rocky Mountains and the Great Lakes
and the doggone Statue of Liberty.

We may fall down as a country sometimes, but we always
get back up. If we don't have hope that we can do it again,
what is the point? Whether big banks are gouging the little people or Ponzi schemes are bilking billions of dollars
out of retirement accounts or whether the unemployment
rate is higher than it has been in decades, Americans still
know how to band together in times of trouble and help
dust each other off. Look at our historical examples: the
Civil War, the Great Depression, 9/11. These and other
catastrophic events in our history were survived, moved
beyond, and eventually prospered from. We didn't just lie
down and give up.

Instead, we gave the rest of the world a peek into the
determination that made us the United States of America
in the first place. Some days it seems we are not much
united about anything. However, our underlying character,
though sometimes hidden under layers of entitlement or
just plain laziness, is still there. America is still the place
that an immigrant can come for safe harbor, not speak a

word of English, create a business from the $11.00 she had in her pockets when she arrived, and become a millionaire—all with a seventh grade education. We are still the country where you can join the military *voluntarily* and serve your country with distinction and honor. Here, whether you are a man or a woman and no matter what your race or socioeconomic background is, you can become a teacher or a lawyer or a doctor or an entrepreneur. Even if it costs you an arm and a leg in student loans. At least you have the choice whether to take out the student loans available to you.

We all need a reminder of the greatness that is inside of us every once in awhile. Even though CNN and MSNBC and all of the other news stations with alphabet soup for names are telling us how we are in the toilet, we don't have to believe them. We can choose to look at all the great things we have going for us. We are the country of innovators and risk-takers. We don't get it right the first thirty-seven times? We will try again for the thirty-eighth. We are not a country of quitters and whiners, though there are some of both of those and they can be obnoxiously loud. That is just white noise, too.

I can't wait until we are the America God created us to be again. If we can come up with the likes of Facebook and iPods and Spanx, we must be awesome. We could all stand to learn a little more about how our government works and those pesky subjects like math and science so we can keep up with other countries, but the bottom line is this: we live in an incredible place. One that I believe will see its true potential again.

"IN GOD WE TRUST" should not just be a motto we notice on our money when an eight-year-old points it out.

For Christians, it should be how we live each day. Do we really trust God? Are we really hoping for the best? Are we prepared for the tough times that we will all inevitably weather? Trusting in God is not an excuse to give up on getting things done ourselves—we still have to do our part. We can, with God's help, turn things around and get back to our former greatness. Maybe even reach a new level of greatness.

We have buffets that stretch for miles so no one in our country should go hungry. We have cities like Las Vegas and New York and Chicago and San Francisco. From coast to coast, there is a place for you where there will be other people that think or dress or believe or act like you. In this great America, my family that is part Asian, part African-American, and part Caucasian can exist.

We put men on the moon, a place 251,968 miles away at its farthest point in orbit. This gives me hope that we will be able to think of a way to rehabilitate our prisoners instead of worry about where the money will come from to build new prisons. We have the Red Cross and Rock 'n Roll, John Wayne and GPS, so it seems entirely possible to me that someday we will come up with good solutions to pollution and homelessness.

This is one amazing place, with our RVs and our seven hundred satellite channels and Diaper Demolishers. We have more opportunity, more land, more freedom than anyplace else I can think of. Name one other country where you can go to a giant warehouse and get a seventy-two-inch plasma television *and* a giant jug of ketchup *and* enough toilet paper to wrap around the entire globe.

God bless America.

Game Changer

A lovely woman named Cindy Pipkin had a brilliant idea several years ago. She's the only person I know who can say her flash of genius occurred while watching an Antonio Banderas movie. The movie, *Take the Lead*, starred Banderas as a ballroom dance instructor. He becomes a teacher in an urban school and gets the kids that no one else wants. He eventually wins them over with ballroom dancing, which he uses as a springboard to mentor them. It made Ms. Cindy dare to ask an important question: why couldn't Oklahoma City have a program like that for forgotten kids? She knew some of our schools were on the bottom of a lot of lists we would rather be on the top of. We needed this.

Somehow Ms. Cindy managed to turn this little seed of an idea into a ballroom dance program for inner city schools. Despite the fact that she wasn't a ballroom dancer. Or had never run a non-profit. Oh, and didn't have any children in the Oklahoma City School District.

Kids that have the deck stacked against them now have two formidable teammates on their side with Ms. Cindy, and her assistant director, Ms. Tami. These are kids that have been forgotten or abused or are at a crossroads. They are near the intersection where one of the next decisions they make can take them down a path of living and change and renewal. Or it can take them down a path of cyclic destruction that perhaps some of their friends or family have chosen. Because of Ms. Cindy's dream, these kids now have a place where they can be good at something. Where they can feel a sense of pride. Where what they are doing is special.

Ms. Cindy knew the name would be of utmost importance. She wanted something that would reflect all of the possibility encompassed within this program. So she named her dream Life Change Ballroom. Isn't that great? Even the name makes me want to get up and start a dance party right now in my jammies.

I am amazed what can happen when someone takes the time to pour good things into kids. Mix encouragement with mentorship and a single semester of ballroom dance instruction and you will turn awkward fifth graders into fearless and graceful dancers. In the beginning, these kids would prefer not to touch each other, almost as if the opposite sex had cooties. Oh, how quickly this will change. The boys usually hem and haw and stare at the floor the first few times they are asked to dance with—gasp!—a girl. They shuffle their feet and mumble under their breaths and won't make eye contact to save their lives.

The instructors, some of whom are volunteers like Mr. Wonderful, are trained in the ways of the dance. They also have a heart for mentoring kids. I have heard Ms. Cindy say on numerous occasions that Life Change Ballroom is a mentorship program disguised by ballroom dancing. The instructors spend a few hours a week with these kids at their schools, and they convince them that (1) it's okay to touch a girl if you are asking her to ballroom dance with you and (2) it's okay to choose a different path than the ones you see all around you.

That's a lot to ask of a program. It's a lot to ask of the kids. For some of these kids the only kind of dancing they've been exposed to is the bump and grind they see on MTV. Or, more specifically, on one of the sister channels of MTV since we all know it no longer plays music videos. These fifth graders are so very worldly. Many of them have already lost the innocence that a ten- or eleven-year-old should have.

Dealing with a parent who is incarcerated or just gone or on drugs can do that to a kid. There are families that have more money than month, or too many mouths to feed. Fifth graders should not be solely responsible for figuring out how to feed and clothe their siblings, but some are. Some of these little kids handle big, grownup issues. You just want to hug the worry off of their little faces and tell them it's all going to be okay, even if you're not sure that's the truth.

Some kids are just going to have to struggle more than others. This concept is hard to wrap my brain around because it seems so unfair. Little kids shouldn't have any heavier burden than what game to play at recess or how to avoid the bully who steals their lunch money, but many do. Life Change Ballroom helps lift those burdens for a few precious hours every week.

The lead instructors of the program teach the boys how to properly talk to a girl and ask her to dance. The kids learn respect and how to treat each other as they are learning the steps. When the music starts thumping, they squeal and squirm with excitement. Instead of some stuffy ballroom dance music, it's usually a song they've heard on the radio. Suddenly the gym floor becomes the dance studio. In some cases, the cafeteria is transformed: tables are pushed against the wall and the smell of tator tots lingers, mixing with that pre-adolescent post-recess funk. The further in the semester it is, the more you see that the students have shed all of their inhibitions when it comes to this new style of dance. They are enjoying the heck out of themselves.

Life Change Ballroom is a game changer for some of these kids. If they enjoy dancing and are pretty good at it, they have the chance to be on the scholarship team, which continues meeting all the way through high school. It provides something that the kids can take pride in when they perform all across the city at public events. It also gives them something to do after school and on weekends. Most of these kids become too busy to get into much trouble. Life Change Ballroom was a game changer for me as well: it's how I met Mr. Wonderful, and it's the whole reason I began living this life.

No one that meets Mr. Wonderful can believe he's a certified ballroom dance instructor. Mostly because he's built like a Mack truck. For a big man, though, he is light on his feet. That man can dance! For my birthday this year—and I won't say which one—he took me out for a very multicultural evening of sushi and salsa dancing. We went to this little Latino club with the teeniest dance floor. This becomes a bit of a logistical problem when you're dancing with a giant, but we still danced until my feet fell off.

Mr. Wonderful and I met at a Life Change Ballroom fundraiser. Our good friends Dennis and Heather witnessed our meeting, and to this day, Heather swears she saw actual sparks fly when we first laid eyes on each other. Honestly, up until then, I didn't know fireworks upon meeting someone were an actual thing. I can now attest to the fact that they are. We danced together all evening and I felt myself melting into the strong, capable arms of this gentle giant. We both knew then that something special was happening.

Our first date following the fundraiser was supposed to be a "dance lesson" but we ended up talking for about four hours and dancing only once. Many of our early dates centered around dancing. Now (if we can get a sitter to wrangle all these kids at our house) we still have a dancing Date Night every once in awhile. Thank goodness for Life Change Ballroom! God knew I had dancing feet and would need a partner for life who could spin me around the dance floor.

There are now twenty-five or twenty-six schools in the program. Every year we go to the annual Life Change Ballroom Dance Competition. I look forward to this evening each year. It's like *Dancing with the Stars* meets *The Bad News Bears* meets *Happy Feet*. It's a real-life story about a group of kids who start out as a rag-tag, rough-around-the-edges bunch searching for their true destiny. By competition time, they have morphed into miniature versions of ballroom dancers. It has all the drama and tears you would expect from any good reality show. These kids have been working all semester on what I consider the fancy dances: foxtrot, waltz, swing, salsa, and the showstopper— The Tango.

Each couple has already competed in a semi-final to have the chance to dance at the annual competition. A local college offers up their performing arts center, including lights and stage and dramatic curtain. The couples picked beforehand from each school dance their little hearts out and legs off. You should see it! They are beyond adorable as they are doing all of these complicated turns and steps and spins to the beat, proof that the rhythm really *is* going to get you.

At the competition, there was a little fifth grade boy that just about broke my heart with his tenderness. All of the boys wear black pants and either a Life Change Ballroom shirt in their school colors or a white tuxedo shirt. This boy was on the small size for his age, and he was on the dance floor with kids several years, and sizes, bigger than he was. His clothes were obviously hand-me-downs. The shirt was so many sizes too large that it was rolled up at the sleeves just to hit his wrists. The pants were cinched up as tight as a too-big belt could make them.

He waltzed his partner—a darling little girl with dark hair all curled and sprayed into an angelic little halo—all around that dance floor like he owned it. His footwork got off a few times, but he just watched the big kids and got right back on the beat. He had confidence. He even had a little swagger. He had learned one of life's most valuable lessons: he has worth. He understood that knowledge is power. He had figured out that the Life Change Ballroom motto, "BE more, DO more, and HAVE more, so they can GIVE more" isn't just fancy words. He knew it was true if he chose to believe it.

This program is still young, so the very first participants are now in high school. Thanks in part to Life Change Ballroom, many of them are on a different and better journey. I believe that's because someone took the time to encourage. To convince them that they could be good at something and have pride in themselves and their skills. When that belief is instilled and tended to and nurtured in a kid, it brings confidence. Confidence, in turn, breeds success.

The same can be said for any of us, even us set-in-our-ways-we-already-know-it-all grownups. Eighty-seven times a day it seems I doubt myself. I wonder why in the world I get up before the butt-crack of dawn when I'm semi-conscious just to write words on my computer. But every day, Mr. Wonderful gets up at the same time I do. He gets his cup of coffee and goes back to our room to get ready while I stare at the computer. And every day, he plants a kiss on top of my head. There's something restorative about that kiss for me. It's a small thing that he does, probably without even thinking about it. But for me, that's the kiss of his confidence in me. Oftentimes I need to be talked down from the ledge of self-doubt that I've stranded myself on. Or propped up like a wilted plant. It doesn't matter if he's just done it. He does it again.

Over and over he shows me, both with words and actions, that he thinks I can do it. He has faith in me, and that helps buoy my confidence whenever it lags. I have always had the seeds of these dreams inside of me. It wasn't until Mr. Wonderful came on the scene and encouraged me that I actually did anything about them.

That's exactly how those Life Change Ballroom kids are. They've always had these abilities inside them—they just needed to be coaxed out. Encouraged into fruition. Eased into being. Kids are so precious. As adults, sometimes we forget how hard it was being a kid. And some of these children have lives that most of us adults couldn't imagine, much less handle.

What if the seed that is planted in some of these kids grows into the idea that they can be the first in their family to not only graduate high school, but to go on to college as well? What if that tiny spark of an idea, the one that just barely catches, turns into a flame of passion for learning that continues to burn brightly their whole lives?

Ms. Cindy was right. Ballroom dancing really can be life changing.

Education

I wish there was a school taught by little kids. Before you think I've lost my mind, hear me out. I think it would help all of us grownup types if we could take a couple of steps back and remember what it was like to be a kid. To live life with joy and meet the day head on with smiles and expectation like kids do.

I know I don't have it all together. In fact, the older I get, the more I realize I need to unlearn some grownup things like worrying and taking moments for granted and hoping life will be something different than it is right now. There are some very important lessons that I forgot somewhere along the way to becoming a grownup.

Being happy just because I get another chance at morning, trying new things, and enjoying every twenty-four hours I have are all ideas I am re-discovering by watching my kids. I don't recall a single time that Big Brother has said, "I really should stop running and playing right this minute." I rarely see Little Brother without a huge grin on his face, even if I can't figure out why he's grinning. And Baby Sister actually bounces up and down, kicking her legs like a soccer player, when she's excited about something. Which is all the time, because she's excited about everything.

I'm learning so much from being the mama to my darling children. This is a whole new kind of education, one that I wish as a grownup I hadn't forgotten in the first place. These kids are teaching me something new every day, and I'm excited to say I almost can't keep up.

Play every day. I watch my kids at the park or church or the doctor's office waiting room. It doesn't seem to matter where we are. They just know how to play. Kids unabashedly find fun things to do with a rock and the teeniest piece of a plastic cup. Whereas I would look at those things and immediately return the rock outside and the plastic to the recycle bin, my kids turn them into walkie-talkies or alien ships or a magic compass.

I'm the worst at getting caught up in the busyness of life. There's a whole laundry list of Things I Should Already Have Done, not to mention actual laundry, waiting for my attention. Then there are the demands of working and juggling three amazing kids and all the chaos of a house with that many children that I tend to use as an excuse. And don't forget Mr. Wonderful—he needs me too. Some days, it's all I can do not to run off and join the circus to be the lady that rides the elephant and wears the fabulous feathery headdress and sequins. She looks like the only care in the world she has is to just look pretty and stay put on that elephant. I'm sure there's more to it than that, but there are days when becoming circus folk doesn't sound too shabby.

When I remember to play, I find that I really enjoy these children God has blessed me with. I enjoy my life. I confess I even enjoy mundane tasks—or at least I don't loathe them as much. For example, I am not crazy about putting away the fourteen piles of laundry that are usually awaiting my attention. I realize laundry seems to be my theme here. Should you take a gander at my laundry room you'd understand why. When all of us work together and have a "Folding Party" while listening to music and dancing all around, I see this as a memory in the making, not just a task to cross through on the To Do List. My kids love to dance with me anytime, anywhere, and there's just something about all that twirling and whirling to the beat that makes us all dissolve in a bundle of giggles.

Spend time with God. We have a collection of crosses hanging on our living room wall. One day as I was walking by, I noticed that one of the crosses—the crucifix one with Jesus on it—was gone. I looked around the entire area but I couldn't find it. So I did the next logical thing. I turned to the kids.

"Not Me" does a lot of naughty things in our house. He/she has been known to eat the cupcake that rendered us one short from the batch for the school party, break the heel on Mama's favorite pair of high heels, and spill an industrial size bottle of bubbles on the back patio making it a slick and hazardous wasteland. I fully expected "Not Me" to make an appearance on this one. Therefore, I was more than a little surprised when Little Brother left without saying a word. After a few minutes, he came back from his room carrying the cross. Aha! I had my culprit.

Having a conversation with a three-year-old is a bit like asking for directions in a foreign country. There's a lot of arm waving and hand gestures and almost everything gets lost in translation. But he said something that I've been thinking about ever since. Though the details are sketchy, when I asked Little Brother why on earth he had the cross and what he was doing with it in his room, he said simply, "I just needed Jesus with me."

Wow. Out of the mouths of babes for sure. What a great thing for a three-year-old to already grasp. Granted, he meant literally, but his faith is so simple and pure it makes me want to bottle it up and open it whenever I need a refresher course in How to Love God. He felt a need to be close to God, so the best way he could think of doing that was to climb up on a bench, get the cross with Jesus on it, and hide it in his bedroom.

Ever since that day, Little Brother understands it's okay with us if he wants to take Jesus with him for a little while. I see them together sometimes, and I love his image of Jesus. I catch Little Brother flying Superhero Jesus around on his cross, making whooshing flying sounds as they fight crime. His Superhero Jesus doesn't have a weapon or cape, but he rights wrongs across the globe. Every once in awhile, I walk by the wall where the crosses are, and when one's missing, I know that Little Brother just needed Jesus with him that day. That missing cross reminds me I should take Jesus with me too.

Have patience with the little things. Patience is a hard-won commodity for me. There are lots of times it's in short supply at my house. I'm ashamed to say that I fall short of being all I can be in the patience department. Especially with the tiny little detail-y things. I'll laugh about how Little Brother flooded the bathroom, and then I completely blow my stack when I see someone's stinky socks on the floor of *my* room. Again. For the four hundredth time.

Kids can exhibit patience for the smallest of things. Like when Big Brother works on his Legos™. Building things that require forty-seven thousand pieces each the size of an atom takes a lot of patience—and he has it in spades. When Little Brother is playing outside, he can dig through the layers of rock and sticks and old leaves until he gets enough mud to create whatever messy sculpture he was aiming for. Don't even get me started on Baby Sister and how she patiently chews her way through every single thing she can find to put in her mouth.

Kids get that sometimes patience is all about the little things. Working for forty-five minutes on opening a child-proof cap is impressive. Spending time every day for three weeks digging a hole the size of Rhode Island in the backyard just to see if the hole can function as a swimming pool is truly something to behold. Working for hours with strips of magazine scraps and glue and poster board to make a "collage" too large to display anywhere but the White House front lawn is a feat in and of itself. Watching my kids do tasks, even the ones that they really shouldn't be doing, has been a learning experience for me about patience.

Get excited about stuff. One thing I adore about kids is how they anticipate things. As grownups, our birthdays seem to come around far too often and that morning alarm begins blaring way too soon. But for kids, counting the days until that special birthday has all the pomp and circumstance as a dinner with the president would or a countdown to the shuttle launch. I love that kids get excited about the ordinary. It doesn't even have to be a birthday. It can be morning or seeing a friend at school or finding a cricket in the bathroom.

I've seen my boys get excited about seeing a helicopter fly overhead. Or discovering all the earthworms that oozed their way out of the dirt after a hard rain. Or when Baby Sister plays a simple game of peek-a-boo. When do we lose our capacity to get excited about the little things? To celebrate the small moments that when combined together make one truly live a joy-filled life? Why don't we celebrate each little victory with the same gusto we reserve for the auspicious occasions? I think it might be okay to do that, right alongside our children.

Let's get physical. When I watch my kids, I'm amazed at how active they are. Have you ever tried to keep up with a child? You will be plumb worn out. There are many reasons why you should do it, but trying to get some physical exercise every day is a good lesson from the kiddos. First of all, it just makes you feel better. Doing a little something to take care of your body gets the blood pumping, helps the self-esteem, makes life a little easier when it comes to bending and lifting. Kids do this all day everyday. At least mine do.

They run from the backyard to the front to school to the neighbor's house to their room, climbing over obstacles and jumping tall building blocks in a single bound. They are dancing to the music one minute and then running sprints to the mailbox the next. Jump up, sit down, roll across the floor, play hopscotch, ride a bike—this is all in the span of three-and-a-half minutes. It's daunting, and I'm not suggesting we try to keep up with them lest we end up in traction. I am just thinking that moving our bodies in some way every day is probably a very good thing.

Be creative. Have you ever noticed how every little kid thinks they're a good artist? Most even think they're great. When is the last time you drew anything other than a doodle in a meeting that was boring you to tears? When is the last time you gave any serious thought to the tough decision between Burnt Sienna and Sepia? Can you remember feeling so confident drawing anything or being artistic in any way?

If you're like most grownups, it's probably been way too long since you've been in touch with your artistic side. Maybe you even wrote yourself off when you were younger. "I could never draw that" or "I'm not really an artsy type." God himself was the greatest artist of all time, making interesting looking animals and painting gorgeous sunsets. Who are we as grownups to take that away from ourselves? It doesn't have to be great, or even good, but getting out the sculpting clay or watercolor paintbrush or playing the piano that you haven't touched in years is getting in the artistic spirit. It feels so good to create, and the more you do it, the better you get. The less you censor yourself.

Make new friends. Kids are great at all sorts of things, and making friends is definitely at the top of the list. They make it look so easy. "Hey, I have a ball, wanna come play?" That's about all it takes. I see my boys meet new kids at the park or the grocery store or the bank or school and I love that they can't imagine that these new kids won't want to play with them. Won't want to be their friends. All they can see is a new possibility in this person they just met. They want to play immediately. I like to consider myself a social butterfly, but I still find myself in situations where there are new people, aka new friends to be made, but something in me shies away.

Maybe it's at the gym and there's a clique of ladies who all workout together. We obviously having working out in common, so why don't I just introduce myself, "Hey, I'm here to workout too, wanna play?" But sometimes I don't. Sometimes I get those thoughts in my head like those ladies are all together and probably don't need anyone else in their group. Or maybe they'll judge me because my kid's wearing his shoes on the wrong feet again and they'll see when they pick up their kids from childcare. Or maybe they won't like me.

It could be a work meeting or a social occasion or just that time at church where you're supposed to introduce yourself to someone you don't know. No matter where it is, it seems like once you become an adult it gets harder and harder to make friends. Taking a lesson from a little kid in how to just dive in and expect people to want to be your friend might help make it easier.

Have confidence. Kids just have that confidence that somehow we adults have lost along the way. They don't worry too much in their early years how they look or if they're wearing the latest trends or if they make enough allowance or whether they go to the right school. I get that they don't have as much to worry about as we do—I mean, we are the ones in charge of the mortgage and the raising of kids and keeping of jobs and all. However, it's still a great lesson to learn that we are okay exactly how we are. We're one of a kind, even as grownups, and that's pretty awesome.

Kids are amazing; even Jesus said so. He wants us all to come to him as children. What does that say about who children are to him? What does it say about us?

Anyone up for a game of hide-and-seek?

Nature Girl

Those who know me know I am not the outdoorsy type. I prefer to enjoy the outdoors by watching the nature channel from the comfort of indoors. At quite a young age, I realized my idea of camping was no hair product in a Motel 6.

Some days, I wish I was an outdoor kind of gal. In my perfect world, I would be Nature Girl, and I would fight all kinds of natural disasters with my sidekick, Oscar the Wonder Dog. Sidebar: Oscar—no surprise here—is also not an outdoorsy type. He will not go outside if it is too wet or too cold, and the one time I let him loose in nature was a disaster. He wandered about twenty feet, got in some poison ivy, and was covered head to tail in burrs that took me an entire afternoon to remove.

Nature Girl is insanely competent, knows how to start a fire (or is it build a fire?), and can find due north at all times. She wears running shoes and cargo pants and looks amazing without a stitch of makeup. People naturally gravitate to her in a forest fire or torrential rain. She never worries about how her hair looks in a ponytail and has a confident stride that says "I can handle anything." She is always appropriately dressed no matter the weather. It is almost as if she has a sixth sense about what the day might hold, or at least, a personal pipeline to the one accurate meteorologist in our area.

I, on the other hand, turn into a drowned rat at the first sign of humidity. Much to my chagrin, I melt in the heat like a stick of butter. I despise all of nature that I consider scary—bugs, rodents of any kind, bears, snakes, and plants that stick to your clothes or make you itchy. I turn into a complete baby at the first sign of inclement weather.

Maybe all of this stems from a bad experience I had when I was five. If I remember correctly, and I'm probably not, my parents enrolled me in this program for young girls that was supposed to help build our self-esteem. All I know is we got together once a week to make arts and crafts, learn songs, and eat snacks. I'm pretty sure I was just there for the snacks, but whatever.

The summer after I joined I went to some sort of day camp. We rode a bus to the campgrounds, sang songs like "Do Your Ears Hang Low," and chattered all the way there. I felt like such a big kid on that bus ride. When we got off the bus at our cabins, there were restrooms (a pre-requisite to my camping experience even then) and rumors that we were having banana splits for our snacks that day. Did I mention that I was there for the snacks?

The day started great—lots of crafty fun and good food and new friends. The plan was that we would go on a hike through the woods, then have snack time and finally, take a short rest before we went home for the day. I just knew this was going to be the best time ever.

The hike was going to be led by our fearless Twelve-Year-Old Girl leader. I remember thinking, "She's so grownup—it's a good thing we have her to lead us through the woods." You might be wondering where the actual grownups were.

Looking back as an adult, I am appalled at my memory of their disappearance, though at the time it never dawned on me to question it.

I have a very vivid memory of seeing a group of the grownups, and when I say grownups, my five-year-old self must have seen these college kids as really old, sitting together behind our cabin smoking some of the strangest cigarettes I had ever seen. Kind of bent and twisted up and strange smelling. Hmmmm. But it was 1981 and my kindergarten experience had not yet prepared me for the realities of life—a twelve-year-old is *not* a grownup and camp counselors should not be smoking marijuana while in charge of kids.

But I digress. Twelve-Year-Old Girl was doing her best to enhance our camping experience. Bless her heart, looking back, she really was trying to make sure her little herd of five-year-old girls had fun. We walked and wandered and looked at leaves and trees and squirrels…for awhile it was complete bliss. And then we started to feel some sprinkles. No worries, little campers! This is all part of the hike! A little rain never hurt anyone!

The sprinkles turned into big fat drops which turned into a scary thunder and lightning show. We were drenched and chilled in our little shorts and T-shirts in no time flat. Like any good leader who knows when to call it quits, Twelve-Year-Old Girl decided we should head back to camp. Except where was camp again? Despite the rain, I had been having fun up to that point. When I heard the panic in her voice, my little five-year-old heart beat with a primal fear. Twelve-Year-Old Girl didn't know where we were? But she's our leader! She's supposed to keep us safe—I want my mommy!!!!!

It seemed like an eternity that we were lost in those woods. I'm sure it was probably only about fifteen minutes, but in kid time, that's about eight months. I was one of the ones wearing sandals. Even then I chose impractical footwear over comfort. At some point, because I am sure the "woods" we were in were about the size of my current backyard, one of the actual grownups found us and led us back to our cabins. We got to have some quiet time and it was warm and our snacks were waiting for us. The rumor was false, by the way. Our snack was chocolate chip cookies.

There were more crazy happenings at that little camp. During naptime on the second day, we heard a strange sound, like a tiny baby rattle. Turns out, somehow a baby rattlesnake was trapped between a screen and the wall in our cabin. I remember the "counselor"—and I use that term loosely now—told us not to worry because it couldn't get out. Only just now am I wondering: where in tarnation was that baby snake's mama? I also have a memory of the "counselor" sending me to get another "counselor" when a girl fell off a bunk bed. Because of the sense of urgency, I did not even take time to put on my sandals. I ran in my bare feet through a sticker patch. If it hadn't been for the bus rides and the snacks, the whole two-day camp would have been a complete nightmare. I am pretty sure this experience scarred me for life when it comes to nature.

Even though sometimes I still long to be that sturdy, efficient, no-nonsense girl, I'm just not. I am starting to be more at peace with the woman God has created me to be, despite my occasional hope that I might magically morph into someone else when I am not looking. I am just me, living in my crazy little chaotic world with twenty tubes of lip gloss and non-practical shoes and air conditioning and only the vaguest sense that I know where I am geographically at any given time.

I am becoming okay with the fact that I have lived in Oklahoma City now for ten years—a lovely, not-too-large town—and yet I can still find myself needing to call Mr. Wonderful for directions. It usually goes something like this: "Hey, honey! I'm by a sign that has a giant rooster on it, and I just passed a street sign that I think had a university in the name. Do you know where I am?"

That's me. With all my craziness and flaws and tons of charm but no sense of direction once I have entered a mall—you would think that would be like the mother ship calling me home, but it's not—I'm learning to accept myself. God created us all, and it has taken the majority of my life for me to feel comfortable in this skin He has given me. I am learning to focus on the best, most true parts of myself. That's so important when the negative self-talk starts to burrow its way into my brain. Instead of wishing to be some other type of person, or worse, comparing myself to an actual person, I try to remember the qualities that make me, me.

For instance, when I am beating myself up about how I don't cook and my poor kids are going to have crazy eating habits because sometimes Mama decides it is okay to eat cereal and leftover Chinese takeout for dinner, I remind myself that I make the World's Best No-Bake Cookies. When I'm feeling blobbish because I have not worked out in four weeks and my pants are feeling tight and I have consumed a surprising amount of cake in one sitting, I look at my gorgeous collection of shoes and tell myself that my feet are prepared for any social occasion. If I start going down the road of "What am I doing with my life?" I look at my office wall to remind myself that my education was a gift I cannot take for granted. I am right where I need to be at this moment in time.

God certainly has his work cut out for Him when it comes to me. I am stubborn in that you-can't-reason-with-me-when-I'm-acting-like-a-two-year-old way. It takes me longer in the mornings to wake up than is natural. I have an insane love of old movies, caffeine, and surfing the internet that He has had to compete with to get my attention. Slowly, God has shown me that He loves me and that He created my unique self to be this exact person. Not some replica of someone else or a version of who I wish I was. But me. Overly sensitive, gentle-spirited, bad hair-day, creative, green-eyed, loving mom with nice top teeth and sweet smile me.

Though sometimes it seems I've just met myself, I am really starting to appreciate the person God made me to be.

Sanctuary

Every mama I know can attest to the fact that every once in awhile we just need two consecutive minutes of peace and quiet. Whether you have one child or nineteen and counting, that is hard to come by.

For instance, today was going to be the day that I could sleep past dawn. You know, really sleep in. The boys were at a sleepover, Mr. Wonderful was at training, and the baby was still sleeping so I settled in for a luxurious extra hour of sleep myself. I had just nestled myself all snug in my bed and was dozing off when there was a loud roar and an actual flash of blinding light in our bedroom. Was it the rapture? Did someone bomb my house? Had I just won America's Got Talent?

When I finally gathered my wits about me, I realized that our house had just been struck by lightning. And now all hell had broken loose with everything that plugged in. Simultaneously our home alarm was going off, the lights on one side of the house didn't work, and the refrigerator was making a weird sound while spurting water intermittently out of the water dispenser onto the floor. It wasn't even 7:00 a.m.! I am ill-equipped to deal with this much mechanical malfeasance when I am well-rested and highly caffeinated, much less when I have been up twice in the night with a newborn and my husband is at a two-week military course. This is all way above my pay grade.

I won't bore you with all the details, but after frantic calls to the alarm company and texts to my husband, my husband's best friend, then my husband again, all while emptying the cup that was catching the refrigerator water, I did manage to get a handle on almost everything. I sit here typing this with only the sound of the refrigerator freaking out and the knowledge that there are still several things in our house that are not working: garage door, internet, phone, satellite, and probably a few other things I have not discovered yet. This is Mr. Wonderful's department, not mine. He is so competent with broken stuff and household repairs that I never worry about this sort of thing. If something happens and he is away, it is like being thrown into a pit full of vipers and dentists and coaches who make you run sprints. Basically, my worst nightmare.

If this had been some sort of crafting emergency or there was legal research that needed to be done RIGHT THIS MINUTE or you needed an answer to a musical question on *Who Wants to Be a Millionaire*, I'm your lifeline, baby. But fixing things and technology just confounds and frustrates me. Before Mr. Wonderful, I would have crawled back into bed to escape a morning like this one. Or I just would have moved.

I am a low-tech kind of gal. I still actually write things down when I want to remember them. Sure, I can use technology. I just can't bend it to my will like some people can. Navigate a computer, yes. Hook one up, no. Big Brother got frustrated with me when he was trying to teach me a game on his portable gaming system. Poor kid, he has no idea that he is going to be programming my DVR once the satellite is up and running.

I *need* a Sanctuary. I need to feel like all is right with my world, even for a few minutes. As a mom of three young kids, there are not many places that fill this need—those little munchkins can find me nearly everywhere. And unless I really did pursue my dream of running away to join the circus, I need a Sanctuary right here in my own home.

As a little kid, when I needed a place to run away I had this amazing playhouse. I was probably about seven when my Grandpa Stanley dreamed it up and built it with his own two hands. He is a lot like Mr. Wonderful—he can fix anything with duct tape and a crescent wrench. A true jack-of-all-trades, he decided to give his grandkids the coolest playhouse anyone had ever seen. It was absolutely majestic, that playhouse. Built from mere plywood and two by fours, it stood like a beacon in the middle of my backyard. That playhouse was my safe haven, my refuge throughout my childhood.

It was not some run-of-the-mill playhouse made in China to be assembled by complicated instructions in four languages. Grandpa had created a one-of-a-kind masterpiece. He decided to put the whole thing on stilts. We could look out the front door of the playhouse and survey the entire neighborhood, spying on whatever unfortunate soul was outside trying to get some yard work done. He even imagined that occasionally we might need an emergency exit. In addition to the stairs with not one, but two landings that led up to our front porch, he also made a rope ladder in case we needed to escape the bad guys.

In the span of one afternoon, that playhouse could be a school or spy headquarters or a flower shop. It was my house and my library. I was constantly rearranging the furniture and dragging toys and dolls and books and sleeping bags out there. We played in that playhouse year-round. Somehow my grandpa knew that even kids need a sanctuary every once in awhile. A place to go and get away from the grownups and homework and crushes gone bad. A place where our imaginations could run away and our friends could have sleepovers and our minds could think kid stuff for awhile.

Memories of that playhouse are some of my best, and they make me long for a grownup playhouse. For now, I have to settle for my bathtub. It is about the only place where I can find peace and quiet and take a minute for some Mama time. Several things have to happen for me to be able to access my Sanctuary, though.

Step 1: put the kids to bed early and threaten with bodily harm if they get out of said bed.

Step 2: make sure Mr. Wonderful is available to run interference to ensure no little person sneaks by our bedroom door.

Step 3: run hot water, grab a glass of wine and a good book.

Step 4: Ahhhhhhhh.

I absolutely love my life, and I know how good I have it. I thank God every single day for a man that was willing to take on all this crazy *with* me and the crazy *of* me. Mr. Wonderful, even in the midst of rough times or disagreements or knock-down-drag-outs, is a partner in every sense of the word. And I am so grateful to have three healthy, smart, beautiful children.

But sometimes Mama just needs a break. We have all heard the saying, "If Mama's happy, everybody's happy."

This could not be more true at our house. If I get a little break every once in awhile where I can mindlessly float away, have some quiet time and a good soak, I am a much better mom. A better wife.

There is nothing like going to my Sanctuary after a rough day. My advice to moms everywhere: whatever it is that fills you with peace and makes you feel like the world should go ahead and keep turning—do that. Not only are you making yourself feel better because you are being kind to yourself, you are helping everyone else around be able to tolerate you. At least, that is how it works at my house. Mr. Wonderful is a sweet and patient man, but even he has his limits. I can tell when he has reached them with me because he is practically pushing me into the tub, forcing a glass of wine in my hand and asking if I need anything to read. This is his way of saying, "Get it together, woman!"

Even after a good day, some Sanctuary time can make it better. We ladies are especially bad at putting ourselves low on the To Do List. We like to take care of everyone but ourselves, oftentimes working to the point where we don't recognize the woman in the mirror anymore. It is high time we all realize that taking care of ourselves is not selfish, it is necessary. As the care-takers and care-givers of our families, we cannot do our jobs well unless we have done a good job of taking a break. Finding balance. Giving ourselves permission to let it all go for a moment. Trust me; it will all be here when you get back.

I really needed my bathtub this morning, but unfortunately I had things to do like call repair people and read our homeowner's insurance policy and give a baby a bottle and work for a living. Too bad life keeps getting in the way of my bathtub time. Rest assured, however, at the next possible opportunity, I will be headed straight to my Sanctuary. I will rest, refresh myself, and replenish some of what life sucks out of me every day.

Do I hear running water?

Part IV

The Toast

A Letter That I Should've Written a Long Time Ago

Dear Mom and Dad,

Don't worry, this isn't a "please send money" letter. Now that I'm a parent, I really just wanted to take to the time to say thanks. You guys turned out to be a lot smarter than I originally thought, and I am so glad that you were the ones who raised me. Looking around at some of the yahoos I could have gotten stuck with, I am especially grateful.

As a mom now myself, I understand that I must have driven you crazy! All the questions, the tears, the drama, the last-minute-I-just-remembered-I-need-four-dozen-cookies-by-tomorrow moments probably made you wonder what in the Sam Hill was wrong with me. Or made it difficult for you to remember why you decided to have kids in the first place.

Mom, it is now clear to me why sometimes I would say "Mom, Mom, Mom, Mom, Mom, Mom, Mom, MOM, MOTHER, BETH, MRS. BEEBY!" just to get your attention. You had the uncanny ability to tune out all of the crazy around you. This was incomprehensible to me as a kid—you didn't want to hear every word I said? Every line of a song that I sang again and again because it was the only line of the song I knew? This was just one weapon in your arsenal of tricks to survive the chaos, and now, having honed this skill to near perfection myself, I get it. You had to do this to save your sanity.

Dad, I appreciate your work ethic and your attempts to instill it in me as well. Your whole "If you're early, you're on time; if you're on time, you're late" theory is still lost on me, but I do manage to arrive most places *approximately* when I need to. And I'm usually *almost* prepared when I do arrive. That's thanks to you.

Parents, I appreciate all of your hard work. I now see for myself how difficult it is to have a job or two, and have three hungry, growing, needy children. Oh, how needy these children can be! They always want to eat and wear clothes and sleep in a warm house. It's exhausting! Thanks for keeping us fed, clothed, and in a really nice home that you somehow managed to pay off on two teachers' salaries even while putting us through college. You guys are a hard act to live up to.

You probably knew this already, but when I was a teen-ager, you both were so embarrassing! There were times I thought I would, like, actually, like, die because of something you did or said in front of my friends. Dad, mowing the lawn in your shorts and black dress socks was enough to send me over the edge, rolling my eyes and threatening to go live with my "real" parents. Now, ironically, my sweet husband often does the same thing, carrying on your tradition. Someday, I hope it will embarrass our kids as much as it did me. But for now, I'm just appreciative of a beautiful yard.

And Mom, your sparkling conversations—in French, no less—made me cringe when I was in high school.

Whose mom does that? I didn't appreciate the fact that you were fluent in several languages like I do now. When you would do your Julia Child impersonation or speak in your British accent, which I'm assuming you knew sounded exactly the same, I usually just told my friends you had had a stroke. I didn't know what to do with that level of shame.

Now I see our children—the oldest rapidly approaching "Tweendom"—and I can already see the eye rolling in my future. There will be a lot of sighs and blank stares from Big Brother. Though it's impossible to know exactly how Little Brother and Baby Sister will navigate their teenage years, I daresay lots of muttering under breaths and slamming of doors and your basic flair for the dramatic will ensue.

I can see that my children will be experiencing many of the same moments I did, and it must fill you with absolute glee. It must feel a little like vindication for all those times we kids forgot to say thank you or broke something you really liked or gave your heartburn for our life decisions. I am not really sure how you survive something like parenthood with all your faculties intact, but kudos to you guys.

Mom and Dad, have you ever thought of writing some sort of parenting manual? I am positive it would be an instant best-seller; I know I would buy it. You had some pretty good ideas. For instance, instead of punishing me right away, you might give me a whole night to sleep on it. I would worry myself into a frenzy that you would indeed be sending me away to a boarding school for my latest infraction. That was genius! Your punishments were almost always fair and they were far less terrifying than the one I had built up in my head.

With three kids, you both had a lot going on. If I wasn't bugging you about how I needed new basketball shoes, then Little Brother Matt was needing a ride to a friend's and Baby Sister Melody was holding her breath until she passed out in the tantrum of all tantrums. Usually in a public place like Wal-Mart or church. Goodness, we must have tested your patience over and over and over and over and over again.

Surprisingly, I don't remember a lot of meltdowns on your part. I say surprisingly because I now see that they would have been entirely justified. I'm taking that from your playbook as well, or at least trying to save my meltdowns for the privacy of our room after the kids have gone to sleep. Looking back, you both were pretty patient in the face of all of the ridiculousness that we put you through, and I'm trying to channel that as well.

I remember Little Brother Matt throwing water balloons at passing cars on a highway, one of which happened to be a police car. I don't remember yelling or name-calling from you guys during the resolution of that situation. Both would have been appropriate in my opinion. I just remember that he didn't do that again.

Dad, I recall that I backed the car over the Christmas lights with which you had so carefully lined our driveway—two years in a row. When I confessed, you just went outside and started cleaning up the broken glass, muttering under your breath about how they really should focus on teaching backing up in Driver's Ed. Again, no yelling or scathing put-downs. Good job on that.

I mess up this parenting thing twenty-seven times a day. Fortunately, I had some great parents whose tried and true methods I can rely on. And I can see you probably borrowed some of those methods from your parents. It's a lot of pressure being in this multi-generational line of good parenting. But in those times when I think about throwing a temper tantrum of my own—breath held, eyes bulging until I pass out—I have your good decisions and history and ideas to lean on. And nearly every time, I don't throw that tantrum.

Parenting is the hardest gig I've ever had, hands down. I hope that when my children get a little older, they will look back on how they were raised and think that there are some things from our playbook that they will borrow when raising their own children.

I know I will probably embarrass the tar out of them, what with my uncanny ability to turn any sentence into a song, the way I occasionally wear my boots with my pajamas when I can't find my house shoes, and the many displays of public affection I participate in with Mr. Wonderful. It will be utterly humiliating for Big Brother when he walks into our house with several of his friends and finds me smooching up a storm with Mr. Wonderful.

Parenting is an interesting ride for sure. Only the strong survive, and thankfully, you guys are some of the strong. Thanks for setting boundaries and bedtimes and making me eat my vegetables and drink my milk at every meal and expecting me to do my best at everything and making me turn in my homework on time and driving me around to every lesson and slumber party and school event. Mom and Dad, thanks for always being there, for trying to use those teachable moments whenever they were presented, for having my back and for making me own up to my mistakes. I hated most of that at the time, but I love it and I'm grateful for it now.

You guys did a great job. I hope and pray that Mr. Wonderful and I can get close to that in raising our own kids. Thanks for all your hard work—I hope you know it was worth it.

I love you both,
Meredith

P.S.   It was me who left the Easter eggs in their basket until the summer sun made them stink to high heaven.

P.P.S.   And sorry I accidentally dented the hood of Mom's car while practicing my *Dukes of Hazzard* roll across the top of it.

I Don't Know Yet

Recently I went in for my yearly lady checkup. I happen to have the most fabulous OB/GYN on the planet. Dr. Mills is actually available for her patients and she doesn't herd you through her offices like cattle through a shoot on sale day. She makes you feel that whatever stupid question you're asking about what's happening to your body isn't stupid at all.

We were chatting—yes, I chat with my gynecologist—about how hard it is to be a mom and a professional at the same time. Now, please don't think I'm slamming stay-at-home moms or non-moms or anyone. I'm specifically addressing one portion of the mom population and my hat's off to all of the others. Please don't send me hate mail.

Anyway. Because she was pregnant with her second child at the same time I was pregnant with my third, I was preaching to the choir. You want to have the best birth experience ever? Go to a doctor that's going through the exact same thing as you and is at your same place in life—professional woman, mom, wife, paying off student loans (I assume), buying a new house, supporting your husband's career while trying to manage your own and still have time for your kids.

The conclusion we came to is that we need wives. Not like a Big Love or Sister Wives polygamist lifestyle kind of thing. Believe me, I don't share or play well with others when it comes to my husband. We decided we just needed someone to do all the little detail-y things around the house that lots of us mamas do, like pay the bills or pick up the kids or do the laundry or mop the floors. To handle all of the stuff some mamas do, you'd have to hire a maid, chauffeur, personal assistant, nanny, and personal trainer. Oh, and a chef. Even though Dr. Mills could probably afford all of that, I, alas, cannot. And you know if a doctor is talking about needing a wife, she's the kind of woman who gets right in the middle of her family and gets her hands dirty. She doesn't expect others to do stuff she wouldn't do herself.

Going from two kids to three meant Mr. Wonderful and I had to change our defensive strategy. No longer could we play a man-to-man defense—we had to switch to a zone. It's difficult sometimes, but it seems to be working. This experience is just reinforcing the fact that being a mom of any sort is really challenging these days. Frankly, anyone brave enough to attempt it deserves a standing ovation. And a one-way ticket to Crazy Town.

Our discussion made me put my thinking cap on, which is good because I've been wrestling with some really big questions lately. Should I move my Roth IRA? Should I grow my bangs out? If I wait much longer to get a haircut that question will be answered for me. And finally, should we have another baby?

Dr. Mills gave me the green light if we're interested in the next few months. I've always wanted a big family, but I like my kids spread out. I don't know how I feel about two kids in diapers at the same time. Wait, yes I do. It's terrify-ing! I also don't know if my sanity can take it. Unfortunately with a looming expiration date on this gal's aging eggs, we don't have the luxury of time. If I want to avoid having a baby at the age of forty, we're going to have to do some fast thinking.

Don't get me wrong. I don't think forty is old. In fact, the older I get, there are lots of ages that I don't find old anymore. My parents are making their sixties look good, so those benchmarks just don't hold the same angst for me as they used to. However, in the world of baby-having, forty is not young. I know famous people and movie stars and art-ists have babies well into their 40s. They also look like they never even carried a child six hours after giving birth, so I can't use them as a realistic measuring stick. Especially as I notice my extra post-pregnancy skin that has apparently hibernated for the winter on my belly. Is it my souvenir from my birth experience? Does it ever go away? I was just kind of hoping it would retract on its own. Instead, I've been busting my humps and lumps at the gym for several months now and it's still here.

Despite the bonus skin it left me, pregnancy was a special time for me. I had never had that experience even though I was Mama to my two sweet boys already. Carrying human life around for nine months made me want to shout from the rooftops, "Hey, everybody! Look at me! I am woman, I am life!" I had to settle for shouting it from street cor-ners though, as my husband wouldn't let me climb anything too high.

I had a great pregnancy, despite those annoying preg-nancy symptoms universal to most women—nausea, extra fat, strange cravings, mood swings, and hormone rushes.

I will probably get hate mail for this, but I actually liked being pregnant. That's why it's so possible for me to think about having another baby.

I just don't know if I want to do it right now. Okay, not right this minute, but in the relatively near future. I've enjoyed feeling like me again. Drinking my lemon drop martinis and eating sushi whenever I feel like it. Being close-ish to fitting into my pre-pregnancy pants. Working out my frustrations on an elliptical at top speeds. This makes me happy. I relish the thought of *not* being the gassiest person in the house. It thrills me to no end that I no longer have to read everything before I ingest it to make sure I'm not doing something dangerous for my baby.

Plus, Mr. Wonderful was the best pregnant gal's husband. That man was so sweet, reassuring me that I was beautiful every step of the way. He attended doctor visits and heard words like placenta and mucous plug and pap smear without turning six shades of green or running away. He held my hand and dried my tears, sometimes while wiping away tears of his own.

Combine the terrific husband, a great birth experience due to copious amounts of drugs, the best doctor, and a biological clock with a broken snooze button—is it any wonder that I'm thinking about it? It's terrifying to think about having four kids of any age, but if we did this relatively soon, we would have four under the age of nine. Three of them would be five and under. Hold on, I have to get a bag to breathe into because that sentence makes me hyperventilate just a little bit. I know babies are a gift from God at any time. I also know that since I'm not a movie star *yet*, sooner is better than later.

If we were blessed with four kids, it would be insanity at first. I'd have my own three ring circus: clowns, tiger tamers and all. On the flip side, as the kids get older, it would be amazing. Cue nostalgic Christmas music and sepia camera lens here. I can picture all four of my kids with their spouses and kids gathered around a beautifully decorated tree, singing carols by candlelight. That image makes for a Rockwell-esque family photo. Which is definitely not my family.

In reality, it would probably be more like loud noises and weird smells. Not to mention spilled cider and sticky messes from attempts at homemade sugar cookies and the baseball Santa gave one of the grandkids going through my plate glass window. I can just see us all moving in slow motion to try and stop it...NOOOOOOOOO!

Time is always of the essence, isn't it? Sometimes we want to fast-forward; sometimes rewind. If Mr. Wonderful and I are going to have four bambinos, we'd best hurry up. I don't want to go for any world records or act all Hollywood about having a baby. Because you never know what life will hand you, it's best to breathe in the right now and hoard those present times as if they are your last. Someday they will be.

Living life loud and full of thunder and purpose and mountain-top moments and mistakes is what it's all about. Having It All seems to be the quest of most women I know. But having it all isn't really about having everything. It's about hand-picking your priorities, placing them in your basket, and hanging onto it with all of your heart.

Ode to Mr. Wonderful

How does a man go about getting a nickname like Mr. Wonderful? I'll tell you how. He takes out the trash without me asking. He wrestles with our kids. He opens my car door for me, cooks amazing meals, and knows how to fix stuff. He occasionally even scrubs toilets.

Notice there was no mention of flowers or chocolate or gifts of diamonds and pearls. The first time Mr. Wonderful took out my trash, I about proposed to him right then and there. It was a little early in our relationship for that, but I swear, I swooned. Old-fashioned, googly eyed young girl swooned. That sort of thing is sexy talk to me.

I do not need a man to give me extravagant gifts or read me poetry in bed. I need a man who will get off his posterior and do things. Recognize the need and fill it. Just take care of stuff in a real-life go-getter sort of way. Mr. Wonderful gets this. I don't know if it is just the kind of guy he is or if he sees how insanely happy it makes me (read: ready to smooch his face off), but I love it! This man had me at Hefty™.

Mr. Wonderful has this great mix of manly and tender. By day, he does his drill-sergeant-military-camouflage-weapons-of-mass-destruction thing, but—I'm not supposed to tell this because it'll ruin his street cred—the man has the heart of a poet. He can fix anything under the sun and sure knows how to handle a power tool. And he looks good doing it. He will come in all sweaty from his fixing of things around the house and smooch my face like he has waited all day for that. He can be absolutely manly in his cursing and muttering and puttering around but then he will do something sweet like write me a song. Thank goodness he quickly realized the utter futility in trying to rhyme anything with the word Meredith.

He is the first to admit that he doesn't always understand why something is important to me, but he also lets me know that if it is important to me, it is important to him. I am sure my histrionics and flair for the dramatic must frustrate the crap out of him. I am probably no easy woman to live with.

By his own admission, Mr. Wonderful is in no way perfect. We argue and fuss and fight, but that is (mostly) bliss to me. He is not afraid to disagree with me and tell me what he actually thinks about any given situation. At first that was a hard pill to swallow. You don't agree with everything I say? I couldn't wrap my mind around this concept.

Then I began to be grateful for a man who would tell me things I didn't want to hear. A man who would care enough about our relationship to tell me the truth about what he thought or needed or wanted. Coming from a past relationship where I was only told what the other person thought I wanted to hear, this is a true gift. I can't always get Mr. Wonderful to talk about his feelings, but it is nice that I can count on him for honesty. I actually believe him when he says he will stay.

I'm not used to someone staying. I mean, I never thought I was the kind of person to get left, but as it turned out, I was. After that, I was a little gun-shy about trusting anyone, and believing that said anyone could be a stayer seemed impossible since only time can tell that particular story.

But Mr. Wonderful works so hard at being transparent. It's almost like he wants me to see through his skin all the way into his heart and soul and mind so that I won't have any doubt that he will still be around fifteen or twenty-five or fifty-five years down the road. After being burned, and I mean first degree, rushed-to-the-burn-unit burned, that is so refreshing. How he has made me trust him after all the trust issues I have been carrying around in my little bag is a true miracle. Bit by bit, truth by truth, empty trash can by empty trash can, he has shown me that he is serious about his commitment.

And COMMITMENT as I have come to think of it—a big, scary word in which expectations are too high and no one can possibly achieve this and how do people do it year after year—is now not quite as scary with Mr. Wonderful in the picture. Don't get me wrong—I am still a big, fat chicken when it comes to being married. Remarried. Sometimes it still makes me feel like I need to breathe into a paper bag.

I am currently experiencing a rebirth of my idea of what COMMITMENT actually is. No longer is it about the pretty, surfacy things like spectacular birthdays or grand gifts that make my friends scream with envy or showy bouquets of flowers. COMMITMENT is about the ugliness of relationships. The grossness. The stuff you hide from everyone else but that you work up the courage to show and go through with the most significant of others.

I can't conceal all my bad habits from Mr. Wonderful. There are just too many. It would be exhausting and take too much time away from my *Sex and The City* reruns. He already knows I sweep dirt, actual and proverbial, under the rug. He understands that I am a lawyer who doesn't like confrontation, I am not a great housekeeper, I don't cook, and our house occasionally has a funky smell. I lose track of time when I'm being artsy-fartsy, and I feed the kids hotdogs for every meal when he is gone. I would love it if he didn't know about my shoe addiction. It would be great if I didn't get crazy hormonal during certain times of the month, and he is bound to see me with my mud mask on eventually. But he doesn't seem to shy away from any of this, despite all of the warts and baggage and sludge I bring to our relationship. For the first time ever, I am allowing—no, inviting—someone into to my deepest, darkest, scariest places.

Now, COMMITMENT means cleaning up our kid's vomit when Mr. Wonderful is bone-tired and all he really wanted to do was catch a quick nap before going to his second job. COMMITMENT is about playing yet another game of hide-and-seek when the man is built like an actual giant and there are only about three places he can fit into to hide. COMMITMENT is taking out the trash, both literally and that of old relationships that his slightly kooky partner brought with her, gently laying to rest each layer of junk and messiness that she has been carting around. COMMITMENT is paying attention and lots of effort and giving her the life she didn't even know she wanted or knew was possible or thought she deserved.

I know Mr. Wonderful and I will experience bad times. I also know that there are so many good times waiting for us that I am afraid sixty years isn't going to be long enough to squeeze them all in. In our relatively short time together, we have already done so much, seen so much, experienced so much, and shared so much of ourselves. Sometimes it feels like we have been together our whole lives. At the same time, it feels like we have so much time to make up for.

Mr. Wonderful is all of the things that I wish I could have told my young self to wait and watch for when choosing a mate. I would tell that young girl that a true partner is one who is present in body, mind, and soul for all the good *and* the bad *and* the boring middle parts that you can't skip over. I would remind her that love is not big expensive flashy gestures or empty promises, but that it is about choosing to love day after day despite the ways your sweetie drives you crazy. I saw a church bulletin once that said love is an action and a choice, not just an emotion. I would say to that girl just hold on. Something so Wonderful is coming your way. It will be big and real and full of God's promises between a husband and wife, and it will fill you up in a way that will take you by surprise.

And I would tell her that his name is Mr. Wonderful.

Saucy

At a recent family gathering, my uncle passed around copies of a picture of my grandma from the 1940s. It was a black and white, taken just after World War II. Grandma's beauty nearly took our collective breath away. Ginger—isn't that a perfect name for a saucy little dish?—has now just turned ninety and is as feisty as she ever was.

I watched her face change as she looked at the picture, remembering the exact moment it was taken. The years melted away, and she was that young girl dating my Grandpa Stanley again. That day they had been out for a leisurely Sunday drive. Doesn't that sound wonderful? Part of me longs to live in a time where a Sunday drive was what young courting couples did. My grandparents lived in a small town, and they had been driving the back roads, talking and getting to know one another.

In the picture, Grandma's about twenty-six. She's dressed in that classic 40s style—knee-length A-line skirt, tailored blouse, dark curly hair pinned back. She's leaning up against the railing of a bridge, casually, as if they were walking along and had the sudden idea to snap the photo right that second. Her hands are in her pockets and her eyes are the tiniest bit squinty, partly from the bright sun and partly from the joy of the moment. She's smiling her familiar smile at my grandpa while he takes the picture.

You can see it's a beautiful day. There is water behind her, and the wind is blowing her hair slightly out of place. I can see pieces of myself in her face, and it's a wonderful notion to me that at that moment in time, she had no idea of the family she and my grandpa would start. She couldn't have imagined back then that she and my grandpa would have two kids, a boy and a girl. These kids would then have several kids of their own who would have several kids of their own. She probably would never have dreamed of the rainbow family that would be her legacy, nor all the jobs and homes and towns and experiences she and my grandpa would have throughout their sixty-three plus years together. And they are still going strong.

Seeing that picture makes me realize two things: it's all going to go by so fast, and I hope that I live a life as full of laughter and love as she has. Grandma has said to me on numerous occasions, the most recent being her ninetieth birthday party, how she can't believe she's not still thirty. She can't believe that her life—the span of nearly a century now—has come and gone so quickly.

Ginger has changed my idea of ninety for sure. She doesn't behave like any other ninety-year-old I've ever seen. In fact, she outpaces most people half her age. She is a shining example of what you can look like as you approach your one hundreth year when you take good care of yourself and follow your passions.

She's a night owl, much like myself. Or at least like I used to be pre-kids. She likes to stay up late and watch old movies—well, what I consider old movies. She probably saw them first run in the theater. When I was in college, I lived with her and my Grandpa Stanley for awhile. We had so much fun! She and I would stay up late together, and I learned a lot about the classics. She is the reason why I know lots of words to lots of musicals: I've seen the movie versions with my grandma.

Of all my family members, she's probably the one I identify with the most. She is a very creative kindred spirit. When Ginger was in her early sixties, she decided to take up oil painting. All of the sudden, she started churning out pictures of flowers and people and sunsets and landscapes. She's quite talented, and her paintings have landed themselves all over the place, my house included.

Grandma Ginger still paints. Every Tuesday, like clockwork, she and my grandpa load up their car and drive thirty-five minutes down the road to Marshall, Oklahoma. This is where they raised my mom and uncle. Marshall is practically a ghost town now. There's no longer even a school in it. It's just a dusty old farming community with a rich history. Of the few remaining old-timer hangers-on that refuse to leave and start again somewhere else, half of them are probably relatives of mine. Marshall has the widest main street in Oklahoma I'm told, and every time I go there, I catch a glimpse of the glory that it once must have had.

On her trips to Marshall, Ginger gathers together with her girlfriends. These are ladies she has known for decades. Talk about your rich history! These ladies are something else. They have named themselves the Pal-ettes, which I find adorable. They show up Tuesday after Tuesday, year after year, decade after decade to paint, talk, laugh, and exchange fashion advice. I'm proud to say that several years ago, I helped introduced Capri pants to the bunch after

I took Grandma shopping and then she showed up at a Tuesday gathering wearing a pair.

These ladies know what true friendship is. They've been through it all over the years: births, deaths, divorce, marriage, sickness, good news and bad. And yet, they paint on, working on new techniques or telling the latest story of what a grandkid—or great-grandkid—did.

I absolutely love the examples that she's set for me. She's my role model that it's never too late to do what you love, what you have a passion for. I think about her now as I get up to write before the rest of my household wakes up. Sometimes I look at that gorgeous young image of her that I keep near my writing space and I remember to just go for it. All of it.

She's shown me that female friendships are important and that to keep them steady, they need consistent nourishment. Sometimes, when I get crazy with the busyness of life, I have a tendency to forget my ladies. These are the women who have seen me through the stuff as well.

I am a founding member of a little club. It's very exclusive because there are only three of us. We have a name and a secret handshake—just kidding, we don't have a secret handshake. Or do we? When all three of us lived in the same town, we would get together for our "meetings" on a fairly regular basis. We called ourselves The Martini Club, or TMC for short.

Kelly and Stephanie and I have been friends for nearly a decade now, a time span I can barely comprehend. We all have kids and Stephanie has moved two-and-a-half hours away, so we can't get together nearly as often as we would like. We try to convene every few months, and we still call ourselves TMC, even though now there are more sippy cups than martini glasses.

The martinis weren't the point of our little club any-way. The friendship was. We formed our own girl tribe, our own way of celebrating, commiserating, and surviving our lives. We've been through it all together—marriages, a divorce, adoptions, law school, births, miscarriages, job changes, moves, buying homes, and selling homes. We've gone through troubles with our bosses, our spouses, our other friends. We've opened our homes and our hearts to each other.

Every woman needs a place to call her own, a friendship that can weather time and distance and babies and the gen-eral craziness of life. This friendship must be a safe place, a hollowed out, hallowed place where you can girl talk one minute and break down the next. We all need someone we can call when things are going great or when things are falling apart.

My dear friend Amy from law school is another such friend. We, too, have been friends for a decade now. Together we survived the fiery pit of hell also known as being a One-L in law school. We did Moot Court, study sessions, gripe sessions, medical tests, moves, adoptions, and everything else in between together. There are moments I wouldn't have survived without her.

I have been blessed with several other circles of friends as well. There are my college friends, my couple friends, my church friends. There are my best friends from high school, my friends from work, my military wife friends, my friends from this chapter of my life. I count myself blessed to have so many groups of friends. These people have seen me at my best and my worst. They are all so dearly trusted that I could call on any one of them, day or night, for a listening ear, a helping hand or a nostalgic conversation.

I think of Ginger and the way she just shows up, rain or shine, every Tuesday. These ladies have collective centuries of wisdom. All of their countless moments are now strung together as pearly reminders on a life well-lived necklace. When they first gather, they spend time painting and catching up. Then they feast on potluck food and great conversation that everyone brings to share. There's always enough left over for any brave husband that tags along. Having been fortunate enough to paint and be embraced in the warm circle of the Pal-ettes, I'm reminded to take time and make it my own. To connect and feast, gossip and hang out, and give my friendships the attention they'll need to stand the test of time like my grandma's have.

Grandma Ginger has also shown me how important it is to take good care of myself if I want to have the kind of ninety that she's having. She's always been petite, and she's always been a fast walker. Even with her little legs, she doesn't wait for you to keep up. You just better hurry. She's a "mall-walker." To my understanding, this is defined as one who gets up early before the mall even opens and walks furious circles around the inside for exercise. I'm pretty sure Ginger laps all of the other mall-walkers.

She eats right, enjoys her dessert, doesn't smoke, and does things she loves. She laughs a lot and has my grandpa to keep her company. You don't have to hang out with them very long to see that they're best friends. They still live on their own, and Grandma drives them everywhere, even on out-of-state road trips. They drive to Texas or Indiana, and Grandma is behind the wheel for every single mile. We get to see pictures when they get back, and they're our link to how our scattered family is doing. Most of us haven't seen some of those relatives in the pictures in years. But my grandparents have.

They're barely slowing down now that they're in their nineties, and I think that's just wonderful. When I grow up, I want to be just like my Grandma Ginger—all saucy and spicy and laughing until tears leak out of my eyes and everyone around me is joining in. I want to scoop out the fleshy, most ripe parts of my life, right down to the rind and savor it. Just like Ginger.

My Pink Champagne Life

I love pink champagne. Probably unnaturally. The way it spills over the glass just makes me happy. I love to feel the bubbles tickle my nose at that sweet moment right before the first sip. Pink champagne just shouts "It's time to celebrate!" Doesn't matter if it's the middle of the week with nothing but bills to pay and To Do Lists to get done. You don't need a holiday or special occasion with pink champagne. It somehow turns an ordinary moment into a par-TAY.

If I'm honest, today's world is anything but a party. It scares me. When I watch the news, all I see is the soul-sucking world of reality television, people doing whatever it takes to get ahead, wars and broken economies, pollution and incomprehensible national debt numbers, drought and devastation and little regard for human welfare. I find it incredibly easy to lose sight of all that I have to be grateful for when I focus on the yuck. Some days it feels nearly impossible to find a reason to celebrate. An excuse to kick up one's heels. A rationale for letting loose, living it up or making merry. Don't get me wrong, I'm not advocating ignorance about the world around us. After all, it is our job to do our best to make our corners better places. But gratitude for all the little things going right is what makes it possible to live what I like to call my Pink Champagne Life.

I haven't always lived this life. There are still days when I am guilty of getting stuck in the mire of bad news. Or continuing to try to be what everyone else wants me to be. Or focusing on all the ways I've failed or forgotten or misstepped. I have been in that dark place where I lost my mojo. My mind. Myself. The place where I gave away so many pieces of me in trying to please everyone else that I had no idea who I was even supposed to be becoming.

That's when all my specialness and deep thoughts and grand ideas were left just barely simmering, forgotten on the back burner of my life. Only when I started being grateful for all of the big *and* small blessings around me did I start figuring out what my Pink Champagne Life could look like. This gratitude helped me remember what it felt like to have grandiose, champagne-just-because-it's-Tuesday dreams and plans. Like Dorothy in *The Wizard of Oz* when the tornado deposits her into Munchkin Land, I started seeing my world in Technicolor again.

Call me Pollyanna or accuse me of wearing rose-colored glasses. I don't care. Now that I've discovered its potential, I don't want to stop living my Pink Champagne Life. And I don't just want this for myself; I want to bring everyone else with me. I'm not talking about ignoring your problems or an absence of them. I just think life would be a lot more bearable if we could find excuses to celebrate the ordinary. Every day, even in the middle of our own wretchedness, wrongfulness, or weirdness, there is usually something to celebrate. Something that will catch your eye or make you catch your breath. Some way to feel like it's all possible, whatever *it* is. God would probably be awfully pleased if

His kids would just look around at the wonder He's created for us and then throw a party. Give a stranger a smile. Or maybe just say thanks every once in awhile.

If you have a hard time finding reasons to let your hair down or kill the fatted calf, so to speak, hang out with a kid. If you don't have one, borrow one, because watching a child for five minutes will remind you that there is plenty to celebrate. Kids allow themselves to use their imaginations, to let creativity take them wherever it will, and to just have fun. I guarantee if you spend time in the company of children, even if they drive you crazy or ask a zillion questions or annoy the daylights out of you because they've put their pants on backward for the twenty-seventh time, you will re-learn how to be grateful for the little things.

In trying to live my Pink Champagne Life, I have made some promises to myself. In the present, and hopefully, in the future, they will remind me how joyous my life is supposed to be. Even in the bad times, I still intend to keep these promises. Maybe especially in the bad times.

I promised that I will no longer live in fear, but I will dare myself to take chances. I will (try to) care less what everyone around me thinks and strive more to figure out what I think. I will take care of my responsibilities and take care of my loved ones. I will also take care of myself. I will trust that within the suitcase of my soul God has placed an abundance of everything that I need for the duration of this journey: joy, persistence, courage, laughter, gladness, helpfulness, creativity, wonder, and patience. I will share those qualities with people around me, and I will share them with myself.

I will laugh more and play more with my kids. I will sing and dance to the music I hear in my heart. I won't complain about the rainy times because they make me appreciate the sunshine. I will love with abandon, and ask to be loved the same. I will finally let go of all the other suitcases I have been carrying for awhile. They are heavy and my journey is long. I will let myself go. I give myself permission to be free in love, in light, in spirit. I will create new and beautiful things without worry or censorship. I will indulge my ideas and the ideas of those around me. I won't let my inner voice or anyone else's judge me.

I will live with joy. I will create for myself and my family a Pink Champagne Life. I will teach them how to celebrate the ordinary moments. I will model this so I can show others it is possible.

Generosity will become my middle name. I will be generous with my time, talents, spirit, and helpfulness, not at the expense of myself but for the betterment of others. I will relish the giving part of myself, and in giving, I will find that I always have more than enough. I will jump up to answer the door when I hear opportunity's knock, rather than pretend I'm not home. I will find more excuses to say yes to that opportunity, even if it is to something that terrifies the snot out of me. I will run, even though I loathe running, toward my best self as if I am an old friend that I can't wait to embrace.

I will encourage in others the beautiful that is already within. I will hold onto all that is dear, and I will let go of all that is not. I will love me, like a mama loves her child, kissing away the hurts and encouraging the chasing of dreams as I grow into this skin of mine.

In making and keeping these promises to myself, for the first time in my grownup life, I am on the cusp of actually becoming the woman I was meant to be. And I am not too much. And I don't shine too brightly or laugh too loudly or wear too much crazy jewelry or animal print or sequins. I am exactly enough for right now.

You are exactly enough.

We are all exactly enough.

And *that* is something to celebrate.

Epilogue

Uncomfortable

Ironically, I was finishing this book about living my Pink Champagne Life during one of the most uncomfortable periods I've ever had. The year 2012 started out with Mr. Wonderful and me doing a Daniel Fast with our church. Basically, you're supposed to eat healthy, unprocessed foods, drink water, and pray for God's guidance over your year, your family, and your church for twenty-one days.

We excitedly participated, giving our year to God and asking him what he wanted to do with this new year. We had barely finished the fast when a tangle of events began unraveling our world as we knew it. In a matter of forty-eight hours, Mr. Wonderful and I were served with papers letting us know we'd be going through a lawsuit this year and we got one of those life-changing phone calls. Mr. Wonderful's brother had died and been brought back to the living; however, the prognosis was poor.

This prompted a 999-mile road trip. One way. With three kids. At the same time, we were supposed to be keeping our house in pristine selling condition (again, with three kids), buying a house, and moving (again, with three kids). By this point, our year had barely begun and we already felt like we were just barely keeping our heads above water.

Then in the summer, my sweet Oscar the Wonder Dog went to be with Jesus, and then in the fall, so did my beloved Grandpa Stanley. Lord, I found myself asking, why all this loss and hurt and confusion? Aren't we following you? My questions were coming faster than the answers during this uncomfortable season turned uncomfortable year. So much turmoil and unsteadiness and that constant feeling of falling and failing. We were becoming disoriented and disjointed, not sure which way was up in this storm of change.

And it just kept raining. Mr. Wonderful received a health diagnosis that will most likely change his career from military man to civilian. Reeling from one major event to the next felt like we were pins in a bowling alley—every hit knocked us down, and as soon as we'd get back up, it was time for the next onslaught.

But we held on. And we held tight to the promises he gave us and to each other. There were many times I dissolved in tears, telling Mr. Wonderful that I couldn't handle one more thing. It seemed as if there was always one more thing.

A strange thing happened as the year wore on though. I somehow found myself becoming more accustomed to that uncomfortable, I-don't-know-where-you're-taking-us-God-but-I'm-just-along-for-the-ride feeling. In the midst of all of the situations we already had going on, we felt that God was also asking us to become foster parents. Oh, and we decided we should have another baby even as we continued to struggle with getting our bearings in our new geography.

But in the midst of it all, God reminded me that pain has a purpose. Pain, if handled the way he wants you to, can lead you to those oh-so-longed-for green pastures and still waters. Even if you don't have the foggiest clue where you are or where you're supposed to be going. Pain could serve not only as a catalyst for change, but it can lead you to the place where God wants you to be. Right within his will.

Looking back with the benefit of hindsight now that this year's nearly over, I see how God has worked everything for his glory. This year has been hard and long and uncomfortable. But at the end of it, I know I'm going to look back and see God's hand guiding and protecting me and my family. Sometimes even carrying us when we haven't been able to carry ourselves.

Thanks to this year, uncomfortableness is no longer something that I fear. It's not even something that I try to avoid. Actually it's made me realize that the last four years of my life have been the most uncomfortable years I've ever had. I'm so grateful for them. Because in being out of my comfort zone, I have learned to embrace whatever's next.

In my old life, I lived very comfortably, safely. I didn't venture too far out of my front door. I lived in fear that things would change. Now, I want to live every day in that disconcerting, who-knows-what-may-happen way. Because that means I'm growing. Changing. Becoming the person God wants me to be and learning the lessons he has for me. It means I am reaching out, stretching out. Just as a mother's body expands and stretches when she houses new life for nine months, my heart and mind have become ever-expanding, ever-changing, sometimes even unrecognizable territories.

So now I don't wish for comfort. Instead, I want to be bold and take risks and make mistakes. Life this year has taught me that it's too short to worry too much about messing things up. I've made thousands of mistakes, and I'll make thousands more. But I don't want to live to regret the chances I never took. I am willing to put myself out there. I am willing to put myself out. I am attempting to fill up every day with the things that are truly important.

Living uncomfortably means I'm never bored. Things are always moving and breathing and morphing and being shaped in ways I never dreamed. Sometimes they're all happening so fast they're one on top of each other, layering my life and my dreams and my moments in different colors and textures. They're an unstoppable flood of change, but I now see that the blessings that follow all of the discomfort are an unstoppable flood as well.

I had to step back many times with only trust carrying me through the situation at hand this year, and that was hard. It meant putting faith into action even though faith is one of those things that's easier to just sit around and talk about. But while I was doing my part to wait and trust, God was doing his part. And his part is *huge*.

The lawsuit went away before we got to trial, and we were blessed by the outcome.

Mr. Wonderful's brother is a living, breathing testament to the power of God. He is alive and well against all odds.

Our nearly two-thousand-mile road trip turned out to be a family vacation we'll never forget.

We survived selling our house, and moving, even with all three kids in tow. Our move to the country—and me becoming a bona fide Country Girl—has brought more peace and joy and love and respite into our home and our family and our spirits. I can watch a sunset or sunrise any day I choose. Deer occasionally wander through our backyard. The stars are visible from my back porch. And coyotes howling at the moon pepper our evenings with nature's song.

I still miss Oscar the Wonder Dog. He didn't get to come with us on our move to the country, and he so would've loved running with the kids out in the woods on the property. Even if he would've been covered in stickers. The hole he left in my heart was a large one to fill, and our new little Bentley Johnny Cash has had quite the time of filling it. But he's doing his best. And somehow, I think he'll end up worming his way into all of our hearts.

The void left by Grandpa Stanley's passing is too big to do anything about except remember how amazing that man was. My sweet Grandma Ginger has lost a little of her spark and verve, but as she allows herself to grieve her friend and confidant and bedmate of nearly sixty-five years, I am hopeful she will stumble upon them along the way. For now, our memories of Grandpa will have to do until we meet again. And I know we are making new ones that Grandpa Stanley is watching from heaven, celebrating with his friends old and new the life that his family continues to carry on in his absence.

We've celebrated a fifth birthday superhero style, all imagination and creativity released through sound effects and action figures. I drank apple pie moonshine with my great-Aunt Frances on her ninety-seventh birthday. I watched my children's faces erupt in joyful wonder at finding a blue-tailed lizard. They ran screaming in delight through the forest that is my new backyard while trying to catch the cottontail whose slumber they disturbed. I decorated my Thanksgiving table with leaves and berries and twigs from my own outdoors. My heart overflowed with gratitude as our houseful of family gathered for prayer.

Of course, there are some things we don't have answers to yet. Things we're still waiting on. Watching for. Wondering how. After nearly half a year of trying to have a baby, we still have a lot of boxes of newborn clothes up in the attic gathering dust until they're needed.

Mr. Wonderful's health situation may pull him out of the military that he has loved and given everything for these past thirteen years. His career and our lives beyond the military are still in flux. We're not sure how this next chapter will look. However, I'm just grateful that his health will still allow him to be my Mr. Wonderful for many, many years to come.

We're at a frustrating standstill with foster family certification until the health stuff and job stuff are worked out. But we continue to believe. And we know that God has plans to prosper us, not to harm us; to give us hope and a future.

And trust comes. Fulfillment comes. Blessings come. Living out your destiny and the life God intended every day can be exhausting and uncomfortable and exhilarating and amazing all at the same time—which is all the more to reason to celebrate every day in my Pink Champagne Life.